Selected Buttons from Other But

BUTTON	BUTTON BAR	FUNCTION
Normal	Font	Cancels character styles
Bold	Font	Formats text as boldface
Underln	Font	Turns on underlining
DblUndln	Font	Turns on double-underlining
Fmt Line	Layout	Displays Line Format dialog box
Fmt Page	Layout	Displays Page Format dialog box
Columns	Layout	Sets text columns
Margins	Layout	Sets left, right, top, and bottom margins
Tab Set	Layout	Displays the Tab Set dialog box
Hdr/Ftr	Layout	Creates and edits headers, footers, and watermarks
Thesaurs	Tools	Opens the Thesaurus
Mac Play	Tools	Plays a selected macro
Mac Rec	Tools	Begins the macro recorder
MergeDef	Tools	Defines a merge for form letters
MergeRun	Tools	Runs a merge to create form letters
DateText	Tools	Inserts the date as text
DateCode	Tools	Inserts the date as a code
Date Fmt	Tools	Selects date format options
Tbl Crt	Tables	Creates a table
Ins Row	Tables	Inserts a row in the current table
Del Row	Tables	Deletes table rows
TColWide	Tables	Changes table column width
Tbl Calc	Tables	Recalculates functions and formulas
Tbl Join	Tables	Combines two consecutive tables

For every kind of computer user, there is a SYBEX book.

All computer users learn in their own way. Some need straightforward and methodical explanations. Others are just too busy for this approach. But no matter what camp you fall into, SYBEX has a book that can help you get the most out of your computer and computer software while learning at your own pace.

Beginners generally want to start at the beginning. The **ABC's** series, with its step-by-step lessons in plain language, helps you build basic skills quickly. Or you might try our **Quick & Easy** series, the friendly, full-color guide.

The **Mastering** and **Understanding** series will tell you everything you need to know about a subject. They're perfect for intermediate and advanced computer users, yet they don't make the mistake of leaving beginners behind.

If you're a busy person and are already comfortable with computers, you can choose from two SYBEX series—**Up & Running** and **Running Start**. The **Up & Running** series gets you started in just 20 lessons. Or you can get two books in one, a step-by-step tutorial and an alpha-betical reference, with our **Running Start** series.

Everyone who uses computer software can also use a computer software reference. SYBEX offers the gamut—from portable **Instant References** to comprehensive **Encyclopedias, Desktop References,** and **Bibles.**

SYBEX even offers special titles on subjects that don't neatly fit a category—like **Tips & Tricks,** the **Shareware Treasure Chests,** and a wide range of books for Macintosh computers and software.

SYBEX books are written by authors who are expert in their subjects. In fact, many make their living as professionals, consultants or teachers in the field of computer software. And their manuscripts are thoroughly reviewed by our technical and editorial staff for accuracy and ease-of-use.

So when you want answers about computers or any popular software package, just help yourself to SYBEX.

For a complete catalog of our publications, please write:

SYBEX Inc.
2021 Challenger Drive
Alameda, CA 94501
Tel: (510) 523-8233/(800) 227-2346 Telex: 336311
Fax: (510) 523-2373

SYBEX is committed to using natural resources wisely to preserve and improve our environment. As a leader in the computer book publishing industry, we are aware that over 40% of America's solid waste is paper. This is why we have been printing the text of books like this one on recycled paper since 1982.

This year our use of recycled paper will result in the saving of more than 15,300 trees. We will lower air pollution effluents by 54,000 pounds, save 6,300,000 gallons of water, and reduce landfill by 2,700 cubic yards.

In choosing a SYBEX book you are not only making a choice for the best in skills and information, you are also choosing to enhance the quality of life for all of us.

The ABC's of WordPerfect 6 for DOS

The ABC's of WordPerfect® 6 for DOS®

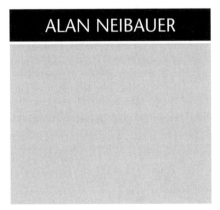

ALAN NEIBAUER

SYBEX®

San Francisco • Paris • Düsseldorf • Soest

ACQUISITIONS EDITOR: Dianne King
ASSOCIATE MANAGING EDITOR: Joanne Cuthbertson
DEVELOPMENTAL EDITOR: Steve Lipson
EDITOR: Brendan Fletcher
PROJECT EDITOR: Kathleen Lattinville
TECHNICAL EDITOR: Tanya Strub
BOOK DESIGNER: Charlotte Carter
PRODUCTION ARTIST: Charlotte Carter
SCREEN GRAPHICS: Cuong Le
TYPESETTER: Thomas Goudie
PROOFREADER/PRODUCTION ASSISTANT: Stephen Kullmann
INDEXER:Ted Laux
COVER DESIGNER: Archer Design
COVER ILLUSTRATOR: Richard Miller
Screen reproductions produced with Collage Plus.

Collage Plus is a trademark of Inner Media Inc.

SYBEX is a registered trademark of SYBEX Inc.

Library of Congress Card Number: 93-84822
ISBN: 0-7821-1177-7

Manufactured in the United States of America
10 9 8 7 6 5 4 3 2 1

To *Barbara Neibauer*

Acknowledgments

Tackling a new release of a major program such as WordPerfect presents its own special difficulties. Doing it while creating a fresh, enhanced format for the ABC's series introduces a second magnitude of challenge. But, as always, the talented SYBEX staff not only met the challenge head-on, but triumphed.

Joanne Cuthbertson, associate managing editor, and Steve Lipson, developmental editor, successfully cultivated this book and the new ABC's format. Brendan Fletcher edited the book, fitting in text and figures and performing his magic with words and phrases. Kathleen Lattinville efficiently coordinated our efforts, tracking our progress and communications between coasts.

My thanks to technical editor Tanya Strub, typesetter Thomas Goudie, proofreader Stephen Kullmann, screen graphics artist Cuong Le, and indexer Ted Laux. The efforts of designer Charlotte Carter translated the concept of this new format to reality. Thanks also to Dianne King and Dr. Rudolph Langer, as well as the other people at SYBEX whose efforts contributed to this book.

My deepest thanks and respect goes to Barbara Neibauer. She has been beside me all along, sometimes pulling, sometimes pushing, but always supporting.

Contents at a Glance

Table of Contents

People thought it just couldn't be done. Improve the world's best-selling word processing program? No way!

If you were one of those people, be prepared for a surprise. WordPerfect has taken the best of version 5.1, added a large dose of extra features, mixed in the power and versatility of a graphical user interface, and presto—a DOS word processor with all of the power of a Windows word processor, but without Windows' hardware overhead and sluggish response.

WordPerfect 6.0 proves that you don't need super-fast computers with extra expensive memory and mega-sized hard drives to get all of the benefits of a graphical user interface. And, if you already use WordPerfect, you don't have to learn a new way of life to become productive.

Equipped with this book, you'll be using WordPerfect 6.0 to prepare all sorts of documents within a few hours, and in ways you never thought possible with a DOS program.

How to Use This Book

Like WordPerfect, this book is an exciting update from a best-seller. We've taken the best features of the renowned SYBEX ABC's series, fine-tuned them for today's busy reader, and mixed in our own blend of tips, tricks, and hints.

You can learn each key WordPerfect function in minutes. Each task is covered in just two pages.

Read the left-hand page for a quick and concise step-by-step guide to how to use the feature. In most cases, you can immediately apply the steps to your own work—you don't have to type some silly document that we've made up for you. (But if you need some more structured practice, you'll find it in this book as well!)

Read the right-hand page to learn useful hints, tips, and tricks about the procedure. Here you'll learn how the function works, some shortcuts, and items to watch out for. Each item is marked with a small icon to help you decide which are important for you to read.

TIP When you see this icon, you'll find a handy tip or shortcut for performing the task.

FOR MORE... When you want some more information, look for this icon. Here, you'll find additional details about the task or a cross-reference to related lessons.

BUTTON BAR This icon means you can perform the function described on the left-hand page quickly using a mouse and the button bar.

RIBBON This icon means you can perform the task described on the left-hand page using a mouse and the ribbon.

Oops! Refer to these notes to troubleshoot problems or to help you when something appears not to work properly.

New! IN 6.0 Features new to WordPerfect 6.0 are explained where you see this icon.

You'll also see a graphic showing what you should look for on the WordPerfect screen.

Before you dive in, be sure to take a look at the "WordPerfect Basics" section that follows this introduction. This short section shows you how to work with WordPerfect menus and dialog boxes and get around in the new graphical interface.

Once you're familiar with the WordPerfect screen, you can use this book in several ways.

— Read from start to finish to learn WordPerfect 6.0 in a linear fashion. And don't worry about slogging through a lot of dense material you don't need—you'll be typing and printing documents in a few minutes!

— Need a quick reference or refresher? Go directly to the left-hand page describing the feature and follow the steps. At the beginning of each lesson is a handy reference showing where you'll read about key features.

— Something not go exactly as planned? Interested in more details? Check out the right-hand page for tips, tricks, or hints.

— Need a little hands-on practice to reinforce your skills? Check out the exercises (**Let's Do It**) after each major Part of the book.

What This Book Contains

We've divided this book into four parts to complement the way you work and learn. In Part One, Quick Start, you'll learn how to start Word-Perfect, type, save, and print documents. You'll learn how to display the WordPerfect button bar and ribbon and how to change your view of your documents. All this and more, in two short lessons!

With the basics under your belt, you'll learn how to edit documents in Part Two. There are lessons on opening documents, deleting and inserting text, correcting mistakes, and moving and copying text. You'll also learn how to insert the date, repeat keystrokes, and zoom the screen to reduce or enlarge the display. There's even a special section on using windows to work with up to nine documents at a time.

Part Three concentrates on formatting. You'll learn how to change the appearance of text and how to insert symbols, icons, and foreign-language characters. There's a lesson on centering text, aligning it at the right margin, changing lines spacing, and setting tabs. Part Three also explains how to add headers, footers, and page numbers, create tables and multicolumn newsletters.

In Part Four you'll learn about some special WordPerfect features. After reading these lessons, you'll be able to add graphic lines and borders, create form letters, and record macros. You'll learn how to check your spelling and how to use the thesaurus and grammar checker to improve your vocabulary and grammar. Finally, you'll learn the basics of desktop publishing—how to add graphics and rotated text to enhance your documents.

At the end of each Part, you'll find some short exercises (**Let's Do It**). These take you step-by-step through a sample document, performing the key tasks described in that Part. Follow the exercises if you're not sure how something should work, or if you want to strengthen your skills before using them in your own documents.

WordPerfect Basics

Working with WordPerfect is really very easy. In fact, if you have a mouse and are at all familiar with graphical interfaces, you'll feel right at home in WordPerfect 6.0. But whether you are a new or experienced WordPerfect user, or whether you have a mouse or not, take a few minutes to read this section.

If you are new to WordPerfect, this section will show you how to communicate with the program using both the text and graphical interfaces. You'll learn about the WordPerfect screen, how to give commands, and how to select options using the mouse, keyboard, menus, and dialog boxes.

If you are an experienced WordPerfect 5.1 user, you'll immediately feel comfortable using WordPerfect 6.0 in its text interface. But don't cheat yourself by ignoring the powerful graphical interface—read this section to see how to take advantage of the new features in version 6.0.

If you have never used a graphical interface before, or do not have a mouse, there's no need to feel intimidated by the following discussion of menus, mice, and dialog boxes. Just take your time working through this section until you feel comfortable with the WordPerfect screen. A little practice will go a long way toward making you a confident WordPerfect user.

Using a Mouse with WordPerfect

While having a mouse is not a necessity with WordPerfect, it certainly makes WordPerfect easier to use. For example, with a mouse, you just point to the function you want to perform and click the left mouse button. A mouse is particularly useful if you use graphics, since it allows you to change the size and position of graphic boxes and lines without even one keystroke!

There are several types of actions you can take with the mouse:

—   The instruction *click* means to place the mouse pointer on an object, then quickly press and release the left mouse button.

—   *Double-click* means to click twice. If you double-click and nothing occurs, then you did not click fast enough—don't wait before each click.

—   To *drag* means to place the mouse pointer on an object, press and hold down the left mouse button, then move the mouse. Do not release the mouse button until you reach a specified location.

One note on using a mouse with WordPerfect: If your mouse doesn't seem to work correctly after installing WordPerfect, select File ➤ Setup ➤ Mouse (if you're not sure how to do this, turn to the sections on working with menus and dialog boxes later in this section). Select the Type option, choose your type of mouse from the list that appears, then select OK.

Using the Keyboard

Though it is certainly easier to use WordPerfect if you have a mouse, you can get by with the keyboard alone. Most commands or actions that can be performed by using the mouse can also be performed with a few keystrokes. In this book, keystrokes that should be pressed together are separated by a plus sign. The combination *Alt+F5*, for example, means that you should press and *hold down* the Alt key, press and release the F5 key, then release the Alt key.

Other key combinations are pressed in sequence, one after the other. These are always separated by commas. For example, *Home, -* means to press and release the Home key, then press and release the hyphen key.

If you are an experienced WordPerfect 5.1 user, you should be aware that some commonly used keystrokes are different in version 6.0. For example, you are probably in the habit of pressing F3 to use the Help system, Esc to repeat keystrokes, and F1 to cancel an action. In version 6.0, these actions are performed by F1, Ctrl+R, and Esc, respectively. To return to the more familiar WordPerfect 5.1 layout, select File ➤ Setup, choose Environment from the pull-down menu, then select *WordPerfect 5.1 keyboard* from the dialog box that appears.

Conventions Used in This Book

Throughout this book you will get concise instructions on how to perform WordPerfect functions. In most cases, you can follow the instructions whether or not you have a mouse.

Most instructions tell you to *select* an option. Selecting an item means to choose it in a way that performs some action. To select an item with the mouse, point to the item with the mouse pointer then *click* the left mouse button. You will soon learn how to select menu and dialog box items with the keyboard.

To *highlight* something means to place the cursor at the option so its name appears in reverse. Highlighting does not perform any action immediately but prepares the option for some action. Highlighting is usually performed with the keyboard to prepare an item for selection. For example, you can highlight a menu bar option without displaying its pull-down menu.

Often, you have to select more than one item to perform a WordPerfect function. Rather than tell you to *Select File, then select Print/Fax, then select Page*, each of the items you must select are separated by the ➤ symbol, as in

Select File ➤ Print/Fax ➤ Page.

This means to select these three items in turn as they appear on the screen.

Many WordPerfect options also have shortcut keys—key combinations that you can press instead of selecting items from the screen. You'll see shortcut keys listed after the select instruction, like this:

Select File ➤ Open (or press Shift+F10).

This means you can either select File then Open, or press Shift+F10. The shortcut keys are most useful if you do not have a mouse. In addition, most of the shortcut keys are the same as those used for earlier versions of WordPerfect. So if you are a WordPerfect 5.1 user without a mouse, you'll find the shortcut keys most efficient.

Understanding the WordPerfect Screen

When you start WordPerfect, you'll see the *menu bar* at the top of the screen and the *status bar* at the bottom of the screen.

The menu bar displays the menus from which you select the commands to work with your documents. The status bar lets you know where the cursor is located in the document:

Doc	The document number (from 1 to 9), depending on which document you are editing
Pg	The number of the page you are currently viewing on the screen
Ln	The distance of the cursor from the top of the page
Pos	The distance of the cursor from the left edge of the page

When you are working on a document that does not yet have a name, the font (size and style of type) being used will appear in the lower left corner of the screen. Once you name a document, its name appears in this position.

The area between the menu and status bars is the text region. The text region is where your document appears as you type.

WordPerfect lets you work in either a text or graphic interface. In the text interface, WordPerfect runs faster, but you will not see exactly how your document will appear when printed. WordPerfect may be a little slower in graphics, but you'll see your text in the style, typeface, and size it will print.

In text view, the *cursor*—a small blinking horizontal line—indicates where the next character you type will appear. You can use either the mouse or the directional arrow keys to move the cursor to the place where you want to type, insert, or delete characters. You can position the cursor directly under a character on the screen.

In graphics view, the cursor is replaced by an *insertion point*, a blinking vertical line. It also shows your location on the screen, but you can only place the insertion point before or after a character on the screen. In this book, we'll use the term *insertion point* exclusively.

If you are using a mouse, you will also see the mouse pointer. In text view, the pointer is a small rectangle; in graphics view it is shaped like an arrow.

Working with Menus

Selecting a menu bar option with the mouse or keyboard displays a *pull-down menu*. A pull-down menu lists specific operations that you can perform. Figure 1, for instance, shows the pull-down menu for the File option. Notice that the first option on the menu is highlighted, or appears in reverse. This means that it is ready to select or activate. In some pull-down menus, certain options may appear gray, or dimmed. These options are not currently available to be selected but must first be activated by performing some other function.

```
File  Edit  View  Layout  Tools  Font  Graphics  Window  Help
New
Open...              Shft+F10
Retrieve...
Close
Save                 Ctrl+F12
Save As...           F10

File Manager...      F5
Master Document      Alt+F5   ▶
Compare Documents Alt+F5   ▶
Summary...

Setup                Shft+F1  ▶

Print/Fax...         Shft+F7
Print Preview...     Shft+F7

Go to Shell...       Ctrl+F1
Exit...              F7
Exit WP...           Home,F7
```
```
Courier 10cpi                    Doc 1 Pg 1 Ln 1" Pos 1"
```

■ *The menu bar shown with pull-down menu for the File option*

If the function has an alternate shortcut key, it will be listed next to the command, such as F10 next to the menu option Save As. Note that on WordPerfect menus, the Shift key is abbreviated Shft.

Other options in pull-down menus contain special symbols. An ellipsis (…) means that selecting the option will display a dialog box containing additional choices from which you must select. Selecting an option with a triangle symbol ( ) will display another pull-down menu. A check mark (✓) next to a menu option shows that it has been turned on, or its option is selected.

Here's how to use menus:

— To display a pull-down menu, click on the option with the left mouse button, or hold down the Alt key and press the underlined letter of the function. (In text view, the selection letter appears in a different color; it is not underlined.)

— To display another pull-down menu, click on another menu bar option, or press the → or ← keys.

— To select a pull-down menu option, click on the option with the mouse button, press the underlined letter, or press the ↓ or ↑ key to highlight the option and press Enter.

— To cancel a menu, click elsewhere on the window or press the Esc key.

Working with Dialog Boxes

Selecting a menu item or performing a function may display a dialog box. A *dialog box* contains additional options and requires some type of input, by either clicking the mouse or typing on the keyboard. While some dialog boxes only present a few options, others can be quite complex. The dialog boxes shown in Figure 2, for example, contain a number of different types of options.

Moving within a Dialog Box

You can move from item to item in a dialog box by clicking the mouse in the item you want to change.

With the keyboard, press Tab to move forward through the options, and Shift+Tab to move backward through the options. You can also press the number next to the item or the underlined letter.

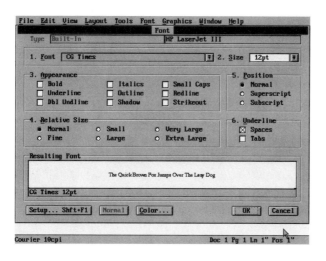

■ *Dialog boxes contain options from which you can select.*

Drop-Down List Boxes

An option that has a ▼ (↓ in text view) on its right contains a drop-down list box. A *drop-down list box* stores several hidden options and displays the currently select option within a long box. Figure 2 shows a dialog box with two drop-down list boxes, the Font and the Size boxes.

To display the list box, click on the ▼, or press the number next to the item, or move to the item and press Enter. When the list appears, select an item by clicking on it with the mouse or by highlighting it with the arrow keys. Remove the list box by double-clicking on the selected item, clicking elsewhere on the screen, or pressing Enter or Esc.

Notice that the box containing the current Font setting is gray, while the current Size box is white. A gray box means that you cannot type an entry directly in the box—you must select from the list. Click on either the option name, setting box, or ▼ to display the list.

You can, however, type a setting in a white box, such as Size. To enter a setting, click on either the option name or the current setting box.

Some list boxes are indicated by both a ▲ and ▼. How this type of list box operates depends on where you click the mouse—on the option name or on the box showing the current setting. If you click on the option name, the list box appears and stays on the screen until you remove it. If you click on the current setting box, you must keep the mouse button pressed down until you select an option from the list—once you release the button the list disappears. With the keyboard, move to the item and press the spacebar to display the list, then select an item from the list.

There is a third type of list box that you may encounter. This type does not drop down but is already displayed on the screen. You can select an option in the box by clicking on it with the mouse or highlighting it with the arrow keys.

Check Boxes

A *check box* is a small square next to an option. When you click on a check box, WordPerfect places an X in the box, indicating that the option is turned on. Clicking on a check box that already contains an X will turn off the option, removing the X. To turn a check box on or off with the keyboard, press the number next to the check box.

In many cases, check boxes are grouped together. Within the group, they are non-exclusive, so you can check more than one box at a time. For example, Figure 2 shows two groups of check boxes—Appearance and Underline. You can click on both the bold and underline check boxes in the Appearance group to print characters that are both boldfaced and underlined.

To turn a check box on or off with the keyboard, press the number next to the group title. Numbers will then appear next to each box in the group—press the number for the desired item within the group.

In text view, check boxes appear as two square brackets: [ ].

Option Buttons

An *option button* is a circle that represents an exclusive setting—only one button in a group can be selected at a time. Selecting one button automatically turns off any other selected.

Figure 2 displays two groups of option buttons—Position and Relative Size. You can only select one option in each group.

You select an option button in the same way as a check box. When the button is turned on, the center circle will be filled in.

In text view, option buttons appear as two parentheses: ( ).

Text Boxes

A *text box* is an area where you can type in information. Move into a text box by clicking it with the mouse, by pressing the number next to the option, or using the Tab, Shift+Tab, or the arrow keys. Then type the value or setting you want for that option.

Some text boxes will have up- and down-pointing arrows on the right. These indicate that you can increase or decrease the value in the box by clicking on the arrows. The arrows are useful if you want to make a small change to the value in the box, such as changing line spacing from 1 to 1.2. To make large changes, it may be faster to simply type the new value yourself.

Commands

Dialog boxes will also contain commands. Selecting a command performs some action immediately.

Most dialog boxes have commands in rectangular buttons labeled *OK* and *Cancel*. Clicking on OK accepts the settings in the dialog box and removes it from the screen. Clicking on Cancel removes the dialog box but ignores any changes you've made. Since it's often easier to work with dialog boxes using the mouse, you will see the instructions *Click on Cancel* and *Click on OK* in this book. If you don't have a mouse or prefer the keyboard, press Esc to accept Cancel. To accept OK, move to the command button so a dotted box surrounds the command word, and press Enter.

Other dialog boxes contain a button labeled *Close* along with a numbered list of command options, such as

1. Select

2. Create

3. Edit

After selecting options from the dialog box, choose Select to accept the settings, or Close to cancel them and return to the document. Remember, you must choose Select to make your settings take effect.

PART

1

Quick Start

Y ou probably already know about the power and popularity of WordPerfect; millions of copies have been sold around the world. Word-Perfect's popularity is well deserved—it is a versatile program that you can use to write everything from letters and reports to newsletters and complete books. What you may not know about WordPerfect is that it is remarkably easy to use.

If you need convincing, just work through the two short lessons in this Part. You'll learn how to start WordPerfect, give it commands and instructions, and write, save, and print documents. If you can learn all this is just two lessons, imagine what you'll accomplish when you're done with this book.

It's So Easy...   See Page...

Lesson 1

Getting Started

The tasks in this lesson will get you started with WordPerfect by teaching you its most basic features. You'll learn how to start Word-Perfect, how to enter text, how to get on-screen help, and more. These are among the most important WordPerfect skills you'll learn, because you will use them with every document you create.

If you have not yet installed WordPerfect on your computer, care-fully follow the installation instructions supplied with the program, then come back to this lesson. If WordPerfect is already on your computer, you're ready to go.

Starting WordPerfect

Starting WordPerfect is easy. Just make sure that you or someone else has installed WordPerfect on your computer's hard drive, and that your computer, monitor, and printer are all set up as they should be.

To start WordPerfect:

1. Turn on your computer and monitor.

2. Respond to the date and time prompts, if they appear.

3. Type **CD \WP60** and press Enter. If you called your Word-Perfect directory something other than WP60, type that name instead.

4. Type **WP** and press Enter. Your screen will look like the figure opposite.

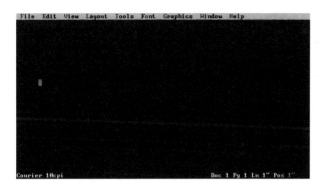

■ *The WordPerfect screen*

 Starting WordPerfect from the root

When you install WordPerfect, it automatically adds the WP60 directory to the DOS PATH command, so unless you or someone has changed this setting, you can start WordPerfect from any directory of your hard disk by simply typing **WP** and pressing Enter.

 Starting WordPerfect with options

There are several options for starting WordPerfect. For example, type **WP /R** and press Enter to speed up WordPerfect by loading parts of it into expanded or extended memory, or type **WP /SA** to temporarily disable network operation. Type **WP /H** to see a list of startup options.

 If you're ready to quit

If you want to exit WordPerfect, select File ➤ Exit, click on No, and click on Yes.

Changing Views

WordPerfect has three views: text view, graphics view, and page view. When you first start WordPerfect, it will be in text view. In text view, all characters are the same size on the screen. In graphics view, you'll see characters and fonts as they will appear when printed. In page view, you'll also see headers, footers, page numbers, and the top and bottom margins.

You can type, edit, and format documents in all three views.

To change to graphics view:

— Select View ➤ Graphics Mode. The figure on the facing page shows a document in graphics view.

To change to text view:

— Select View ➤ Text Mode.

To change to page view:

— Select View ➤ Page Mode.

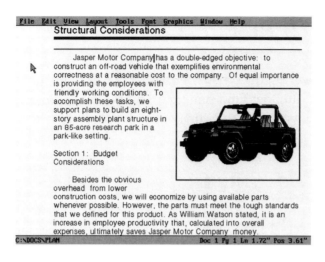

File   Edit   View   Layout   Tools   Font   Graphics   Window   Help
Structural Considerations

Jasper Motor Company has a double-edged objective: to construct an off-road vehicle that exemplifies environmental correctness at a reasonable cost to the company. Of equal importance is providing the employees with friendly working conditions. To accomplish these tasks, we support plans to build an eight-story assembly plant structure in an 85-acre research park in a park-like setting.

Section 1: Budget Considerations

Besides the obvious overhead from lower construction costs, we will economize by using available parts whenever possible. However, the parts must meet the tough standards that we defined for this product. As William Watson stated, it is an increase in employee productivity that, calculated into overall expenses, ultimately saves Jasper Motor Company money.

C:\DOCS\PLAN   Doc 1 Pg 1 Ln 1.72" Pos 3.61"

■ *A document in graphics view*

TIP   ## In a hurry? Use text view

WordPerfect may respond to your keystrokes more slowly in graphics and page views than in text view. If you find graphics and page views too slow, type the bulk of your document in text view, then change to graphics or page view for final editing and fine-tuning.

TIP   ## Like an elephant

When you exit WordPerfect, it remembers the currently active view. The next time you start WordPerfect, that view will automatically be used.

BUTTON BAR   ## Quick change

Click on GrphMode to change to graphics view. Click on TextMode to change back to text view.

Typing in WordPerfect

If you've ever used a typewriter, you'll feel at home in WordPerfect. All of the letter, number, and punctuation keys on the four middle rows of the keyboard work just the same.

To type a document:

1. Press Tab to insert a tab at the start of a paragraph.

2. Type until you reach the end of the paragraph. Do not press Enter when you reach the end of a line. WordPerfect senses when the word you are typing will not fit in the line and moves the word to the next line automatically, as shown in the figure.

3. Press Enter to end a paragraph or to insert a blank line.

4. Press Backspace to erase mistakes.

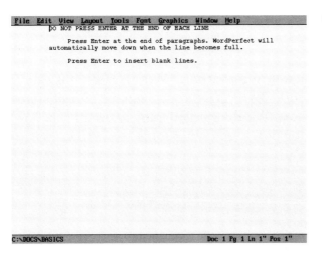

File Edit View Layout Tools Font Graphics Window Help
DO NOT PRESS ENTER AT THE END OF EACH LINE

Press Enter at the end of paragraphs. WordPerfect will
automatically move down when the line becomes full.

Press Enter to insert blank lines.

C:\DOCS\BASICS   Doc 1 Pg 1 Ln 1" Pos 1"

■ *WordPerfect moved the word automatically to the next line as it was typed*

Read what you need

 TIP   ## When you fill the screen...

As you type, the insertion point (cursor) moves down the page and the Ln indicator in the status line changes. As you pass the last line on the screen, the lines at the top scroll up out of view into the computer's memory. You can use the scroll bars to bring the text back down into view. See "Displaying and Using Scroll Bars" in Lesson 3 for more information.

 TIP   ## Is there still room on the page?

When you reach the end of a page, just continue typing—WordPerfect automatically starts a new page, a line appears across the screen, and the Pg indicator in the status line increases by one.

 FOR MORE...   ## Taking control of pages

If you want to end one page and begin another before WordPerfect changes pages automatically, press Ctrl+Enter. See "Inserting Page Breaks" in Lesson 6 for more information.

Getting Help

With a program as powerful as WordPerfect, it is easy to forget how some features work. To help jog your memory, WordPerfect has an on-screen Help system. WordPerfect Help includes information on menu commands, dialog boxes, and other tools.

To get help from WordPerfect:

1. Select Help to display the Help pull-down menu.

2. Select Index to display a list of topics for which help is available. Your screen will look like the figure on the facing page.

3. To see detailed information, do one of the following:

    — Double-click on a subject you want help with—scroll the list if necessary.

    — Press ↑ or ↓ to highlight the term you want help with and press Enter.

    — Click on the Name Search button, type the first characters of the topic you want help on, and when the list scrolls to that topic, double-click on the topic.

4. Select Cancel to exit Help and to return to the document.

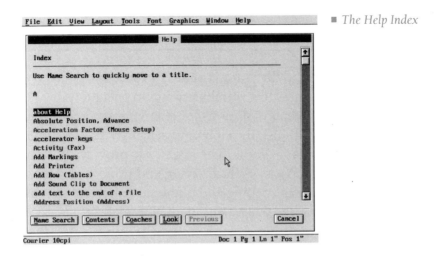

The Help Index

Skip the menu, full speed ahead

WordPerfect also has context-sensitive help you can use at any time by pressing the F1 key. Just display the menu or dialog box you want help on, highlight the item, and press F1. WordPerfect will respond with a screenful of help on the highlighted item.

I know it's around here somewhere!

If you have lost your keyboard template, you can print a copy from within the Help system. Select Help ➤ Contents ➤ Template to display the template. Make sure your printer is on and ready, then press Shift+PrtSc to get a printed copy of the template. Shift+PrtSc may not work if you are on a network.

For more help

Words in Help windows that are underlined (or appear in a different color) are called *glossary terms*. Double-clicking on a glossary term brings up its definition. Words that are in bold are called *jump terms*. Double-clicking on a jump term displays a screen of related help information.

Displaying the Ribbon and Button Bar

The ribbon and the button bar are two special on-screen elements, new to version 6, designed to streamline common operations in WordPerfect.

The *ribbon* displays options for changing the appearance of text in a document. You can use the ribbon to select styles, set columns and tabs, align text, and change fonts. The *button bar* provides buttons for performing common functions, such as saving and printing documents, changing views, and checking spelling and grammar. Clicking on a button is the same as choosing the equivalent menu command.

To work with the ribbon:

1. Select View ➤ Ribbon to display the ribbon.

2. Click on the list box associated with the option you want to change, then drag the mouse pointer to select the desired setting. Click on Tab to set tabs.

3. To turn off the ribbon, select View ➤ Ribbon.

To work with the button bar:

1. Select View ➤ Button Bar to display the button bar.

2. Click on the button of the desired function.

3. Click on the ▼ button on the left of the button bar to scroll additional buttons into view. The ▲ button will scroll the buttons back to their original positions.

4. To turn off the button bar, select View ➤ Button Bar.

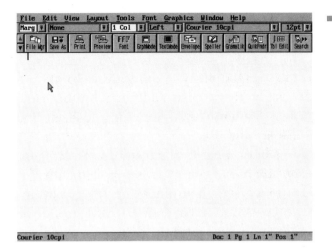

■ *The ribbon and the button bar*

FOR MORE... **But I don't like it there**

You can change the position and appearance of the button bar and create custom button bars. See "Selecting Button Bar Options" in Lesson 17 for more information.

TIP **It remembers!**

WordPerfect remembers the screen appearance when you exit. If the ribbon and button bar were on screen when you last exited WordPerfect, they will appear automatically the next time you turn it on.

RIBBON **Don't waste your time**

The Zoom command in the ribbon (the button labeled Marg) lets you reduce or expand the displayed magnification. In text view, the Zoom option has no effect. See "Zooming the Screen" in Lesson 6 for more information.

Selecting Button Bars

WordPerfect has far too many useful features to fit on to one button bar. Since buttons are so easy to use, additional button bars are available for performing other frequently used functions. Just select which button bar you want to display and use.

Select the Fonts button bar to change the style, size, and color of text; the Macros button bar to run macros supplied with WordPerfect; the Outline button bar to work with outlines; the Tables button bar to change and edit tables; the Tools button bar to use writing tools, work with macros, perform merges and sorts, enter the date, link spreadsheets and use sounds; and WPMAIN to use the default button bar.

To select a button bar:

1. Select View ➤ Button Bar Setup ➤ Select to display a list of available button bars, as in the figure.

2. Double-click on the button bar you want, or highlight it and choose Select. The selected button bar will appear on the screen. If all of the bar's buttons fit on the screen, the ▼ and ▲ symbols on the left of the bar will be grayed.

3. To remove the button bar, select View ➤ Button Bar.

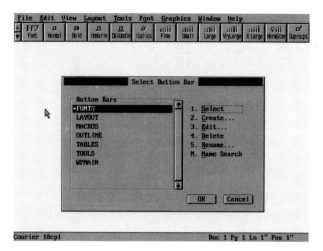

■ *The Select Button Bar dialog box with the Fonts button bar displayed in the background*

Read what you need

🔘 **TIP** **WordPerfect remembers**

If you turn off the button bar—by selecting View ➤ Button Bar—WordPerfect remembers which button bar was active. That same bar will appear when you next select View ➤ Button Bar. To choose the default button bar again, select View ➤ Button Bar Setup ➤ Select, then double-click on WPMAIN.

 For more information

See later lessons to learn about the functions performed by these button bars.

It's so easy...

Saving and
Printing
Documents

W hen you are done creating a document, you need to
print it or save it to disk for permanent storage. Usually you'll do both.
Printouts are convenient for reviewing or distributing your documents,
but you still need to save a document if you want to edit or print it later.

Saving a Document

When you save a document for the first time, you must give it a name. Document names can be from one to eight characters long.

To save your document for the first time:

1. Select File ➤ Save As (or press F10) to display the Save As dialog box, as shown in the figure.

2. Type a name for your document. When WordPerfect saves a document, it does not automatically add an extension. If you want an extension, separate it from the file name with a period, as in

`MYFIRST.DOC`

3. Click on OK.

Once you have saved your document, you can save it again (after making changes) by selecting File ➤ Save.

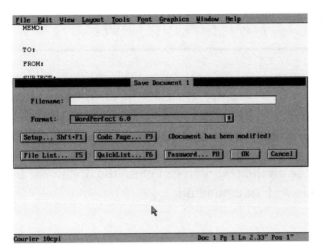

Read
what
you
need

 TIP   ### If you still use 5.1

WordPerfect 6.0 saves documents in a format incompatible with earlier versions of WordPerfect. If you want to use the document with Word-Perfect 5.1 as well, select File ➤ Save As, pull down the Format list box, and select WordPerfect 5.1/5.2 from the list of formats. To change the default saving format (the one WordPerfect uses automatically), select File ➤ Save As ➤ Setup, then select a new default format from the dialog box that appears.

Oops!   ### Don't be lazy

WordPerfect saves a temporary copy of your document every ten minutes. This is only a safeguard in the event of a power or computer failure. *You must still save your document yourself before exiting WordPerfect.*

 BUTTON BAR   ### Make saving simple

 Click on the Save As button to save a document.

Clearing a Document from Memory

Saving a document does not remove it from the screen and erase it from your computer's memory. Instead, the document stays on screen so you can continue working on it.

If you have already saved one document and want to work on another, or if you have changed your mind about what you've already typed and want to erase all the text, you can erase the document from memory by using the File ➤ Exit command.

To clear the typing window:

1. Select File ➤ Exit (or press F7) to display the Exit dialog box, as shown in the figure.

2. Click on Yes to save the document, No not to save it, Save As to change its name or format, or click on Cancel to cancel the operation and return to the document.

3. A dialog box will appear asking if you want to exit Word-Perfect.

4. Select No to clear the window and remain in WordPerfect.

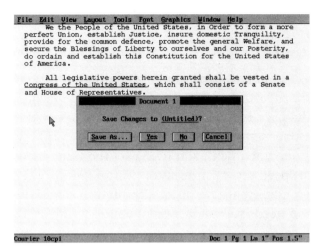

■ *The Exit dialog box*

 TIP ## Still like the keyboard?

The keystrokes F7, N, N still quickly clear the screen without saving, as they did in WordPerfect 5.1. Press F7, Y, N to save the document and clear the screen.

 TIP ## Did I save it or not?

If the document has been changed, the Exit dialog box will contain the message "Document has been modified" and the Yes option will be selected. This is WordPerfect's way of warning you to save the document unless you want to lose your changes.If the document has not changed, the No option will be selected.

 TIP ## Closing a document

To clear the screen after saving a document, select File ➤ Close.

Printing Documents

WordPerfect has many powerful printing features. If you use the default settings, WordPerfect will print every page in your document. You can also print the page you're working on, a bit of selected text, or a series of selected pages. By setting the Number of Copies option, you can print multiple copies of a document, and if you set the Generated By option to Printer, you can speed up the process of printing multiple copies. You can even print a document that's on disk, without ever displaying it.

But if all you need is a quick copy of your document, the process is easy.

To print a document:

1. Make sure that your printer is turned on and ready and that you have paper.

2. Select File ➤ Print/Fax to display the Print dialog box, as shown in the figure. If you want to print something other than every page in the document, click the appropriate options in this box.

3. Click on Print.

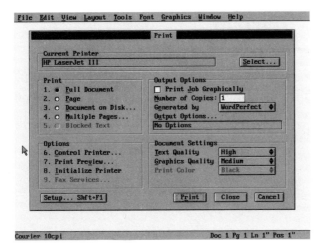

■ *The Print dialog box*

 TIP **Just to be safe, save!**

You do not have to save a document before you print it. However, get into the habit of saving documents whether you print them or not. You may print a document, then need it again at some later time.

 Is that the doorbell?

Depending on your printer and paper feed, you may hear a beep and see the message "Press Shift+F7, 6 to resume printing." Make sure your printer is ready, insert a sheet of paper, then press Shift+F7, 6, G to continue printing.

 One-click printing

 Click on the Print button to print a document.

Selecting Your Printer

If your document does not print accurately, you may have the wrong printer selected for printing with WordPerfect. WordPerfect can print with almost any printer on the market, so if you currently have the wrong one selected, changing it is a simple matter.

■ To select your printer:

1. Select File ➤ Print/Fax to open the Print dialog box.

2. Click on the Select button to see a list of printers installed with WordPerfect, as shown in the figure.

3. Select the printer that is connected to your system.

4. Click on Select.

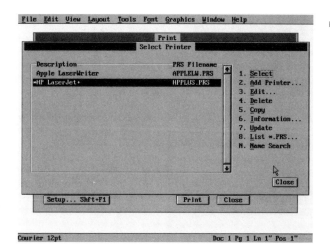

■ *The Select Printer dialog box*

 Your printer isn't listed

If you did not set up your printer when you installed WordPerfect, run the WordPerfect Install program and select the Device option.

 What printer?

If you cannot find your printer model, try selecting a compatible brand. For dot-matrix printers, try an Epson or IBM Graphics printer. For a laser printer, try one of the HP LaserJet models. If you cannot find a substitute, contact WordPerfect Corporation for updated drivers and printer information.

Saving Documents and Quitting WordPerfect

You can save a document and exit WordPerfect using one dialog box. Use this feature only if you are ready to quit WordPerfect.

To exit WordPerfect:

1. Select File ➤ Exit WP (or press Home, F7) to display the Exit WordPerfect dialog box, as shown in the figure. An X under the Save column indicates that the document has not been saved since you last modified it.

2. Click on the Save and Exit button to save the document then exit WordPerfect. If the document has not been modified, no X will appear in the Save column and the default option will be Exit.

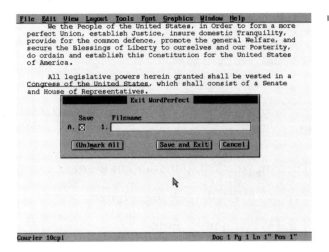

■ *The Exit WordPerfect dialog box*

Read what you need

But I really don't want it

If you do not want to save the document when you exit WordPerfect, click on the X to delete it from the Save column. Click on (Un)mark All to toggle all X indicators on and off.

Using F7 to exit WordPerfect

You can press F7, Y, Y to save a named document and exit WordPerfect. Press F7, N, Y to exit WordPerfect without saving the document.

Let's Do It!

Here is a brief exercise so you can try out creating, saving, and printing a document:

1. Turn on your computer and monitor.

2. Type **CD\WP60**, then press Enter.

3. Type **WP** and press Enter.

4. Select View ➤ Graphics Mode.

5. Press Tab to indent the first paragraph.

6. Type the following text. Remember, do not press Enter when you reach the end of the line.

   ```
   We the People of the United States, in Order to
   form a more perfect Union, establish Justice,
   insure domestic Tranquility, provide for the
   common defence, promote the general Welfare, and
   secure the Blessings of Liberty to ourselves
   and our Posterity, do ordain and establish this
   Constitution for the United States of America.
   ```

7. Press Enter twice—once to end the paragraph and a second time to insert a blank line between paragraphs.

8. Type the following:

   ```
   All legislative powers herein granted shall be
   vested in a Congress of the United States, which
   shall consist of a Senate and House of
   Representatives.
   ```

Now let's save the document under the name HISTORY.

9. Select File ➤ Save As (F10).

10. Type **HISTORY**.

11. Select OK. The completed text is shown in Figure 1.1.

Now, print the document.

12. Select File ➤ Print/Fax.

13. Click on Print or press Enter.

Finally, let's exit WordPerfect.

14. Select File ➤ Exit WP.

15. Click on Exit.

That's all there is to it!

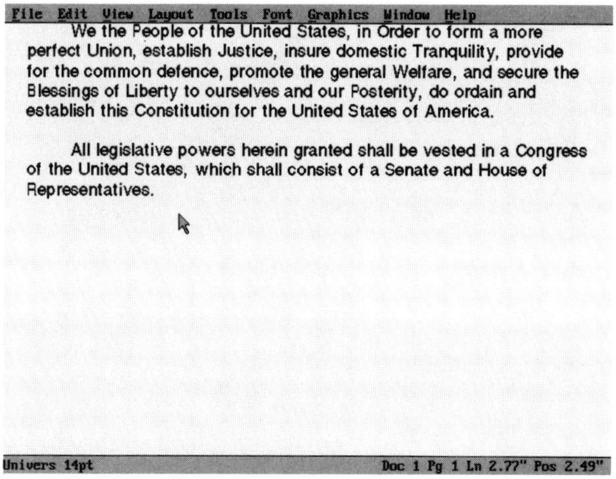

■ FIGURE 1.1:
*The completed
sample text*

PART

2

Editing Your Work

Wouldn't it be great if we did everything correctly the first time around? We wouldn't need erasers on pencils, little white bottles of correction fluid, or the power to impeach the President of the United States. But life just isn't that generous.

Fortunately, WordPerfect is (almost). It can't prevent you from making mistakes, but it does let you change and improve your work before you commit it to paper. In the lessons that follow, you'll learn all about editing your documents. You'll learn how to delete unwanted text, insert new text, and how to get the most out of WordPerfect's graphic interface.

L e s s o n 3

Recalling Documents for Editing

One of the best things about word processing is that you can edit (change) a document as much as you want before printing it. You can print as many draft copies as you want and fine-tune the document until it is perfect—then print the final copy. In this lesson, you'll learn how to open documents you've saved and use some of WordPerfect's basic editing techniques.

Opening a Document

You can edit new documents as you type them, or you can edit existing documents already saved on disk. To edit an existing document, you must first *open* it, or recall it from the disk.

■ *To open a document:*

1. Select File ➤ Open (or press Shift+F10). WordPerfect displays the Open Document dialog box, as shown in the figure.

2. Type the name of the document you want to work on. (Note: WordPerfect expects your documents to be in the WPDOCS directory.) If the document is in a different directory, be sure to type the correct drive and path before the file name. For example, typing **C:\MYFILES\LETTER** would open the file LETTER from the MYFILES directory on drive C.

3. Click on OK.

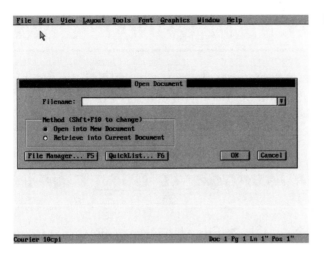

■ *The Open Document dialog box*

File not found!

A message will appear if the file you are trying to open cannot be found. Press Enter to clear the message, make sure the path and file name are correct, then try again. If you still get the message, use the File Manager to view your files, as described on the next page.

 TIP ## Open versus Retrieve

Selecting Open from the File menu starts a new document window. When you select Retrieve, the document is inserted in the current document already displayed.

 ## If your screen goes blank

When you open a document created with an earlier version of WordPerfect, it is first converted for version 6.0. If there is not enough computer memory available for this process, WordPerfect temporarily goes to DOS and you screen may go blank for a few seconds. Just be patient.

Opening a Document Using File Manager

If you cannot remember the name or path of the file, or if you want to see a list of all available files, you can use File Manager to open your documents.

▪ To use File Manager to open a document:

1. Select File ➤ File Manager (or press F5) to display the Specify File Manager List dialog box.

2. Click on OK to accept the default directory; or type the complete path of another directory, including its drive letter. A directory of the disk will appear on the screen, as in the figure.

3. Double-click on the file you wish to open; or highlight the file, then click on Open into New Document.

You can press Esc to exit File Manager at any time.

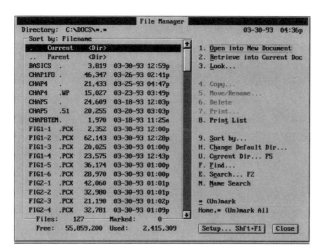

■ *The File Manager
window*

 TIP   If you don't want to type the path

Read
what
you
need

To see a visual representation of the directory structure, press F8 to display a
directory tree. You can double-click on any directory you want to view.

 **FOR
MORE...**   To use the scroll bar

The File Manager box has a vertical scroll bar. For help on using scroll
bars, see "Displaying and Using Scroll Bars" later in this lesson.

 TIP   Viewing documents in File Manager

If you're not sure what a document contains, you can temporarily display
its contents. Just highlight a file in the directory list and select Look.
Click on Next to display the file listed after the one on the screen, Previous to display the one before it, or Open to open the file.

 **BUTTON
BAR**   Find files fast

 Click on File Mgr to open File Manager.

Inserting Text

To insert characters in text you've already typed, you must move the insertion point to the area of the document you want to change. When you enter characters within existing text, words to the right will move over to make room.

To move the insertion point:

— Place the mouse pointer where you want to enter, delete, or revise text, and then click the left button. (In text view, you must place the cursor under a character or space. In graphics view, you must place the insertion point either before or after a character.)

You can also use the keyboard to move the insertion point. The figure on the next page lists some of the most used cursor-movement keys and their functions.

To scroll the screen:

To move the insertion point to a part of the document that is not in the displayed region, you must scroll the screen.

— Hold down the right button, drag the pointer to the edge of the screen, then drag further in the direction you want to scroll.

■ *The cursor-movement keys*

Press...	To move...
→, ←, ↓, ↑	In the direction of the arrow
Home, Home, ↓	To the end of the document
PgUp (PgDn)	To the top of the next (previous) page in the document
Home, ↓ (↑)	To the bottom (top) of the screen or, if already there, displays the next 24 lines of text
Home, ↓ (↑)	To the bottom (top) of the screen, or to display the next (previous) screen of text
End	To the end of the current line

Read
what
you
need

 I thought you said it would insert

By default, WordPerfect is in the *Insert* mode. If you press the Ins key (the 0 key on the keypad), the word *Typeover* will appear in the lower left corner. New characters typed will now replace existing ones.

 All I get is numbers

If you press an arrow key and a number appears on the screen, press the Num Lock key. This turns off the numeric function.

 Splitting paragraphs

To split a single paragraph in two, place the insertion point where you want the new paragraph to begin, then press Enter. Press Enter a second time to create a blank line between paragraphs. Press Tab to indent the paragraph.

Using Scroll Bars

As your document grows longer, it becomes time-consuming to scroll using the mouse. To save time, you can display and use scroll bars to move through a document.

To display and use scroll bars:

1. To display the vertical scroll bar, select View ➤ Vertical Scroll Bar.

2. To display the horizontal scroll bar, select View ➤ Horizontal Scroll Bar. The figure on the facing page shows both scroll bars.

3. To scroll line by line, click the up or down arrow on the end of the scroll bar.

4. To scroll screen by screen, click above or below the scroll box—the box within the bar, between the up and down arrows.

5. To scroll to a different part of the document, drag the scroll box. For example, drag the scroll box to the middle of the scroll bar to display text in the middle of the document.

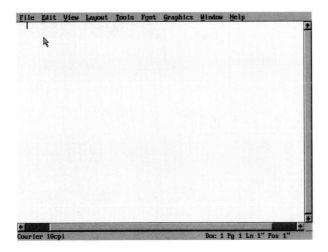

■ *Vertical and horizontal scroll bars*

 **New feature**

Scroll bars are new in version 6.0.

 Is it vertical or horizontal?

Display and use the vertical scroll bar to move up and down through a document.

 Why do I need a horizontal scroll bar?

You only need the horizontal scroll bar when you cannot see the entire line on the screen. See "Zooming the Screen" in Lesson 6 for more information.

It's So Easy...

Lesson 4

Editing Techniques

T he ability to edit a document is what gives word processing its power and versatility. You can type a document, letting your thoughts flow onto the screen, without having to worry about mistakes or the arrangements of your ideas on the page. Then, when you've gotten your ideas out, you can go back over the document and edit it into the final form.

Selecting Text

In order to perform most editing functions, you must first select, or *highlight*, text, which makes the characters appear light on a dark background. Once you select text, you can easily delete it, copy it, move it to another location, or change its appearance.

For example, to apply any of the formats in the Font menu (such as bold or underline) to existing text, you must select the text first, then choose the format from the Font menu. There are two ways to select text.

To select text by dragging the mouse:

1. Place the mouse pointer at one end of the text.

2. Hold down the left mouse button and move the mouse pointer over the text you want to select.

3. Release the mouse button.

To select text with the pull-down menus:

1. Place the cursor in the sentence, paragraph, or page you want to select.

2. Select Edit ➤ Select or press Ctrl+F4 to display the Move dialog box, as shown in the figure.

3. Select Sentence, Paragraph, or Page.

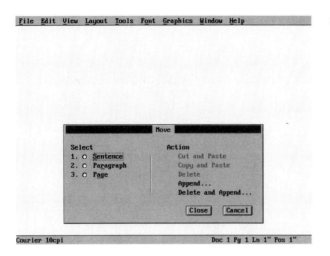

■ The Move dialog box

Selecting with the keyboard

If you don't like using the mouse, you can select text with the keyboard. Place the insertion point at one end of the text and press F12 or Alt+F4, or select Edit ➤ Block. Move the cursor with the arrow keys or type a letter—the block will extend to the first occurrence of that letter.

Changing your mind

To deselect all highlighted text quickly, click the mouse, or press F12, or press Alt+F4. If you drag over more text than you intended to, drag the pointer back over the text you don't want to select before releasing the mouse button.

Printing selected portions of your document

To print only part of a document, select the text you want to print, then select File ➤ Print and click on Print.

Deleting Text

WordPerfect provides many ways to delete characters, or erase mistakes.

▪ *To erase characters:*

— To erase characters to the left of the insertion point, press the Backspace key.

— To erase a character to the right of the insertion point, press the Del key.

▪ *To delete sections of text:*

1. Select the text you wish to delete.

2. Press Del.

The table on the facing page shows more deletion commands.

■ *Some deletion commands*

Press...	To delete...
Ctrl+End	Every character on the line to the right of the cursor
Ctrl+PgDn, Y	The remainder of the page
Home, Backspace	From the cursor position to the start of the word
Home, Del	From the cursor position to the end of the word
Ctrl+Backspace or Ctrl+Del	A word at the cursor position

Read what you need

 So many choices

After selecting text, you can also delete it by selecting Edit ➤ Cut or by pressing Ctrl+F4 and selecting Delete.

Oops! **Watch those spaces**

When deleting text within a sentence, make sure you do not delete spaces between remaining words.

 Deleting blank lines

To delete a blank line, place the insertion point before the line and press Del, or place it after the line and press Backspace. You can use this method to join two paragraphs into one.

Using Undelete

If you erase text by mistake, you may be able to restore it without retyping. WordPerfect remembers the last three deletions you made—whether you used the Del or Backspace key or selected Delete from the Move dialog box.

To restore deleted text:

1. Select Edit ➤ Undelete (or press Esc) to display the Undelete dialog box, as shown in the figure. The last characters you deleted will reappear highlighted at the position of the cursor.

2. Select Restore to restore the text at that location on the screen, or select Previous once or twice to cycle back to the two previous deletions.

■ *The Undelete dialog box*

 I can't get it back!

Undelete will not restore text erased by selecting Edit ➤ Cut. To restore such text, see "Using Undo" on the next page.

 Restoring text in its original location

To restore the text at its original position, first move the insertion point to where you deleted the text.

 Making duplicate copies

Restoring text does not remove it from WordPerfect's memory. You can restore it again—to make a copy of it—as long as it is one of the last three deletions made. For other ways to copy text, see "Copying Text" in Lesson 5.

Using Undo

The Undo command cancels the last editing or formatting you performed on your document. You can use Undo to delete the last bit of text you wrote, delete text you just restored by mistake, return recently formatted text to its original condition, or reverse just about any WordPerfect operation.

To undo your last action:

— Select Edit ➤ Undo (or press Ctrl+Z), as shown in the figure.

You can select Undo again to cancel the last Undo operation.

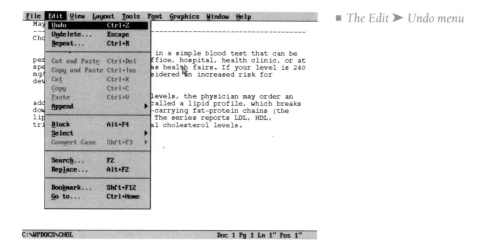

■ *The Edit ➤ Undo menu*

How Undo restores text

Undo restores deleted text in its original location, even if you moved the insertion point.

Always try Undo first

If you delete text by selecting Edit ➤ Cut, you cannot restore it with the Undelete command. If you do try to use the Undelete command, you will no longer be able to restore it using Undo. So, try using Undo first to restore text. If the correct text is not restored, just select Undo again to cancel the operation.

Undelete versus Undo

When you use the Del key or Ctrl+F4 and the Delete menu selection to delete text, the text is stored in an "undelete" area that can hold the last three deletions. You can restore this text by selecting Edit ➤ Undelete (or pressing Esc). Text deleted using Edit ➤ Cut is stored in a separate retrieval area, which can only hold one deletion. Restore the text using Edit ➤ Undo or Edit ➤ Paste.

Searching for Text

If you spend a lot of time scrolling through documents looking for a particular word or phrase, you can save time by using WordPerfect's Search feature. WordPerfect can search an entire document for a specific set of characters in seconds.

To locate specific text:

1. Move the insertion point to the location where you want the search to begin.

2. Select Edit ➤ Search (or press F2) to display the Search dialog box.

3. Type the word or phrase you want to locate.

4. Click on Search (or press F2) to begin the search.

WordPerfect will move the insertion point following the text. If the text is not found, a dialog box appears with the message "Not Found." Click on OK or press Enter to remove the dialog box—the insertion point will be in its original position.

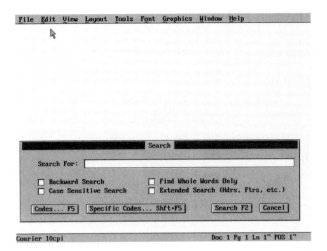

■ *The Search dialog box*

 TIP ### Search options

Select Backward Search if the text you want to search for is before the cursor position. Select Case Sensitive Search to match the case of the characters as you enter them in the Search For text box. Select Find Whole Words Only to locate only entire words that match the search text, not just the characters themselves. Select Extended Search to search headers, footers, and footnotes as well as the document text.

 TIP ### Searching for codes

To locate a formatting code, do one of the following from within the Search dialog box: Press the formatting keystroke (such as F8 to locate underlining) when in the Search For text box, choose Codes to select from a list of codes, or choose Specific Codes to select from a list of codes that require specific settings.

Replacing Text Automatically

Have you ever misspelled the same word several times in one document or realized that you entered the wrong information in several places? Or do you have a certain document that could easily be modified for another use if the same word were changed several times—for example, a letter that could be used another time if you just changed *he* to *she?*

In situations like these, you can use the Replace command to automatically locate any text and replace it with something else.

To replace text automatically:

1. Move the insertion point to the location where you want the search to begin.

2. Select Edit ➤ Replace (or press Alt+F2) to display the Search and Replace dialog box, as shown in the figure.

3. Type the text you wish to replace, then press Enter.

4. Type the text you want to insert.

5. Click on Replace (or press F2).

6. A dialog box will appear reporting the numbers of matching occurrences found and the number of replacements made. Click on OK to remove the dialog box.

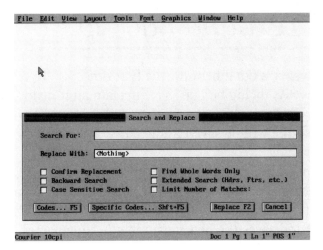

■ *The Search and Replace dialog box*

 Where did it all go?

Don't forget to type something in the Replace With box. If you leave the default, <Nothing>, WordPerfect will *delete* the text it locates.

 Save your document first

Save your document before making an automatic replacement. If the wrong text is replaced, or deleted, clear the screen and reopen the document.

 Additional replacement options

Select Confirm Replacement to have WordPerfect pause before each replacement and display a confirmation dialog box. Click on Yes to make the replacement, No to move to the next occurrence of the text, Replace All to change to automatic replacement, or Cancel. To replace a specific number of matching occurrences, select Limit Number of Matches and enter the number desired.

Saving Edited Text and Backup Copies

When you save a document for the first time, you have to enter its name in the Save As dialog box. To save it again after making changes, select File ➤ Save—this time, the Save As dialog box will not appear, and the changed file will be saved immediately, overwriting the original version.

If you want to use the Save command but keep the original version on the disk unchanged, you can set WordPerfect to make backup copies. Then when you save a document, WordPerfect gives the original copy the extension .BK! and saves the new version with same name.

By default, WordPerfect makes *timed backups* of your document every 10 minutes so you won't lose too much work if your machine goes haywire before you've had a chance to save the document. You can change this option as your needs require.

To change backup options:

1. Select File ➤ Setup ➤ Environment.

2. Select Backup Options to see the Backup dialog box, as shown in the figure.

3. Enter the interval for making timed, or automatic, backups.

4. Select Backup Original Document (.BK!) on Save or Exit to make backup copies when you save or exit a document.

5. Click on OK twice to return to the document.

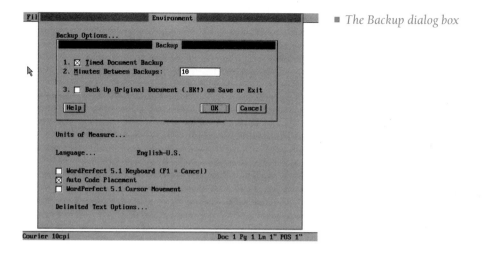

■ *The Backup dialog box*

**Read
what
you
need**

  TIP   **Don't rely on timed backups!**

You must still save your document before exiting WordPerfect, even if a
timed backup has just occurred. When WordPerfect makes a timed
backup, it saves your document in a temporary file. (A small dialog box
appears when the backup is being made.) This file is automatically deleted when you save the document or exit WordPerfect without saving it.
If someone accidentally turns off your computer while you are working in
WordPerfect, however, the temporary file will remain on the disk. The
next time you start WordPerfect, you'll see a dialog box asking if you
want to rename, delete, or open the backup file.

■ TIP   **One generation of backup files only**

If you save a document once, then save it a second time after changing
it, the original backup is replaced by the new version. If you want to keep
the original version unchanged, save it under a new name before editing
it. Select File ➤ Save As, type the new name you wish the file to have, and
then click on OK.

It's So Easy... See Page...

Lesson 5

Moving and Copying Text

S electing text gives you the ability to work with sections of your document as blocks. You already know how to delete and print selected portions of a document. In this lesson, you'll learn how to move, copy, and save selections, and how to append portions to an existing document on your disk.

Moving Text with the Mouse

When you *move* text, you delete it from one location in a document and place it at another. The quickest way to move text is by using the mouse to *drag and drop*. This means you drag the text to where you want it to appear, then drop it in its new location.

You can use drag and drop to move text anywhere in the document, even to a location that has already scrolled off the screen.

▪ To move text:

1. Select the text you want to move.

2. Place the mouse pointer on the selected text, then press and hold down the left mouse button. The message "Release mouse button to move block" appears on the status line, and an icon of a block of text appears alongside the pointer.

3. Drag the mouse pointer to the location where you want to insert the text. The screen will scroll if you move the pointer to the top or bottom of the screen.

4. Release the mouse button.

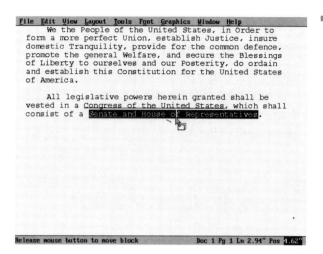

```
 File  Edit  View  Layout  Tools  Font  Graphics  Window  Help
      We the People of the United States, in Order to
 form a more perfect Union, establish Justice, insure
 domestic Tranquility, provide for the common defence,
 promote the general Welfare, and secure the Blessings
 of Liberty to ourselves and our Posterity, do ordain
 and establish this Constitution for the United States
 of America.

      All legislative powers herein granted shall be
 vested in a Congress of the United States, which shall
 consist of a Senate and House of Representatives.




 Release mouse button to move block           Doc 1 Pg 1 Ln 2.94" Pos 4.62"
```

■ *Text ready to be moved with drag and drop*

  TIP   ## Moving text off the screen

In graphics view, the screen may scroll very slowly if you move text to a location not visible on the screen. Switch to text view before moving the text, or use the Cut and Paste on the Edit menu, as described later in this lesson.

Oops!   ## Change your mind?

The text isn't actually moved until you release the mouse button. If you decide not to move the text after you begin dragging the mouse, move the pointer back onto the selected text and release the mouse. If you change your mind after releasing the mouse, select Edit ➤ Undo (or press Ctrl+Z).

FOR MORE...   ## Moving text to another document

To move text to another document, see "Moving Text between Documents" in Lesson 7.

Copying Text with the Mouse

When you *copy* text, you insert a duplicate of it at another location. The original text is not deleted from the document. You can copy text using drag and drop, in a procedure almost identical to that for moving text. The only difference is that you must press the Ctrl key.

To copy text by drag and drop:

1. Select the text you want to copy.

2. Place the mouse pointer on the selected text, then press and hold down the left mouse button.

3. Drag the mouser point to the location where you want to insert the text.

4. Press and hold down the Ctrl key. The message on the status line changes to "Release mouse button to copy block."

5. Release the mouse button.

```
 File  Edit  View  Layout  Tools  Font  Graphics  Window  Help
 This text will be copied.
```

■ *Text ready to be copied with drag and drop*

```
Release mouse button to copy block              Doc 1 Pg 1 Ln 1" Pos 2.6"
```

Read what you need

💡 **TIP**   **Copy or move?**

As long as you do not release the mouse button, you can either move or copy the selected text. Press the Ctrl key to copy the text; release it to move the text. So if you decide to move, rather than copy, the text, release the Ctrl key before releasing the mouse button. If you decide not to copy the text after all, release the mouse button and select Edit ➤ Undo (or press Ctrl+Z).

FOR MORE...   **Copying text to another document**

To copy text to another document, see "Moving Text between Documents" in Lesson 7.

Moving Text with Cut and Paste

While drag and drop is convenient, you may want to move text using the Cut and Paste command on the Edit menu instead. Scrolling a long document while holding down the mouse pointer can be tiresome. In addition, you'll need to use Cut and Paste if you want to move text to another document.

◻ To cut and paste text

1. Select the text you want to move.

2. Select Edit ➤ Cut and Paste (or press Ctrl+Del). The text disappears from the screen and the status line displays

   `Move cursor; press Enter to retrieve`

   as shown in the figure.

3. Position the insertion point where you want to place the text.

4. To insert the text, do one of the following: Press Enter, select Edit ➤ Paste, or press Ctrl+V. If you decide not to move the text, you can place the insertion point at its original location and press Enter to reinsert it. If you decide to delete the text, rather than move it, press Esc.

You can also use the Move dialog box to select a portion of text and use the Cut and Paste command at one time. Just place the insertion point in the text you want to select, press Ctrl+F4, then select Sentence, Paragraph, or Page. Then select Cut and Paste from the right side of the dialog box.

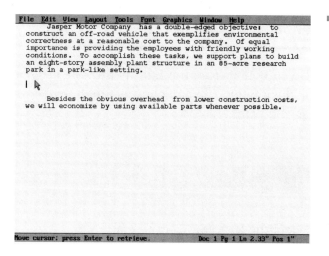

■ *Status line indicating that text is ready to be moved*

 Pasting multiple copies

Cut text will remain in WordPerfect's memory until you cut (or copy) other text—pasting the text does not remove it from memory. To insert another copy of the text at some other location, move the insertion point, then select Edit ➤ Paste again.

 Cut versus Cut and Paste

If you select Edit ➤ Cut, the text will be deleted but the "Move cursor" prompt will not appear in the status line. To insert the text elsewhere, position the insertion point and select Edit ➤ Paste.

 Moving text to another document

To move text to another document, see "Moving Text between Documents" in Lesson 7.

Read what you need

Copying Text with Copy and Paste

You can also copy text from the Edit menu. The original text is not deleted from the document. You can copy as much text as you want, and as many times as you want.

▪ *To copy and paste text:*

1. Select the text you want to copy.

2. Select Edit ➤ Copy and Paste (or press Ctrl+Ins). The high-light disappears around the text and the status line changes to:

   ```
   Move cursor; press Enter to retrieve
   ```

3. Position the insertion point where you want to place a duplicate of the text. Press Esc if you decide not to copy the text.

4. Press Enter or select Edit ➤ Paste (or press Ctrl+V).

You can also copy selected text using the Move dialog box—just select Edit ➤ Move or press Ctrl+F4, and select the appropriate options. The figure shows how the Move dialog box appears when text is selected.

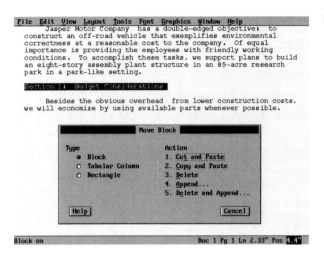

■ *The Move dialog box with text selected*

 Making multiple copies

To insert another copy of the text at some other location, move the insertion point, then select Edit ➤ Paste again.

 Copy versus Copy and Paste

If you select Edit ➤ Copy, the "Move cursor" prompt will not appear in the status line. To insert the text elsewhere, position the cursor, then select Edit ➤ Paste.

 Copying text to another document

To copy text to another document, see "Moving Text between Documents" in Lesson 7.

Saving Selected Text

Sometimes as you write you create a phrase or paragraph that you know you can use somewhere else. Rather than leaving it embedded in the current document, you can save the text as a separate file on the disk. Just be sure to store the saved text with a new name. If you give it the name of an existing document, the original will be replaced.

To save a portion of text:

1. Select the text you want to save.

2. Select File ➤ Save As (or press F10) to display the Save Block dialog box.

3. Type the name you wish to save the highlighted text under.

4. Click on OK.

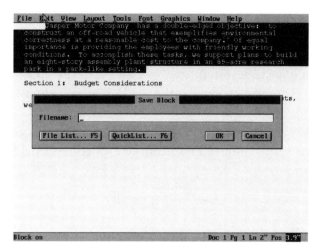

■ *The Save Block dialog box*

Oops! **That certainly seems like a long file name**

You can type up to 67 characters in the Filename box, but only the first eight characters will be used.

TIP **Duplicate file names**

If there already is a document with the same file name that you gave the selected text, you will be asked if you want to replace it. Select No, then enter another file name.

TIP **Where did the formatting go?**

Only the text and codes within the highlighted block are saved. The formatting codes outside of the block, even those that would affect it when printed, are not included in the saved document. To learn more about codes, see "Working with Codes" in Lesson 6.

Appending Text to a Document

When you *append* selected text, you add it to the end of an existing document. If the document does not exist, a new document will be created.

You can use the Append command to form a collection of commonly used paragraphs, or to make an addition to a document that you are editing separately.

To append text:

1. Select the text you want to append.

2. Select Edit ➤ Append to display the options *To File* and *To Clipboard*.

3. Select To File to display the Append To dialog box, as shown in the figure.

4. Type the name of the document to which you want to add the selected text.

5. Click on OK.

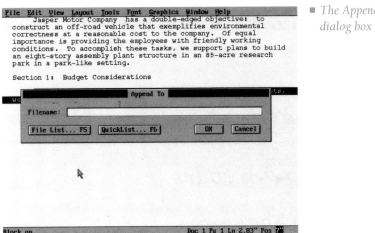

The Append To dialog box

  TIP   **Can't remember the file name?**

If you're not sure which file you want to append the text to, click on the File List button (or press F5) in the Append To dialog box to see a list of files on your disk.

  TIP   **Is this Windows?**

The Clipboard option is only valid if you start WordPerfect using Shell, a program in the WPC60DOS directory. With Shell, you can run up to nine programs at a time, switch between them, and copy information from program to program using the Clipboard. For more information on Shell, refer to your WordPerfect documentation.

  TIP   **Saving and deleting text in one step**

You can use the Move dialog box if you want to automatically delete text after you save or append it. Select the text, press Ctrl+F4 to display the Move dialog box, and select Delete and Append. Enter the file name and click on OK. The selected text will be appended to the document specified and deleted from the document you are working on.

It's So Easy...   See Page...

Lesson 6

Fine-Tuning Your Documents

The editing techniques you've learned so far are sufficient for most simple editing, but you'll also want to take advantage of Word-Perfect's comprehensive array of special editing capabilities. You may not use the techniques you'll learn in this lesson for every short note you write, but they are invaluable for fine-tuning your documents.

Working with Codes

Keys such as Tab and Enter do not display any characters on the screen, even though they affect the format of the text. They do, however, insert invisible codes that can be deleted just like other characters.

To see which codes are in your document, and to delete individual codes, you reveal them in a separate window at the bottom of the screen.

To reveal codes:

— Select View ➤ Reveal Codes (or press Alt+F3). Your screen will look much like the figure on the facing page.

If you want to leave codes revealed as you continue writing, you can, but you'll see fewer lines of text and WordPerfect may be a little slow to respond to your keystrokes.

To remove the display of codes:

— Select View ➤ Reveal Codes again (or press Alt+F3).

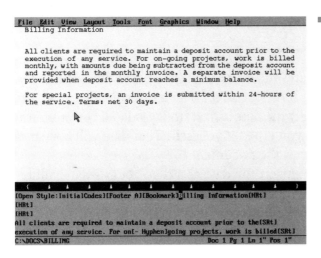

■ *The WordPerfect screen with codes revealed*

Read what you need

When things go wrong

You should reveal codes whenever the text on the screen just doesn't appear correct. You may have entered a code accidentally by pressing the wrong function key.

Common codes

As you use WordPerfect you'll become familiar with the important codes. In the Reveal Codes screen, the position of the cursor is shown highlighted. Hard carriage returns (created by pressing the Enter key) are represented by [HRt], soft carriage returns (added by word wrap) are shown as [SRt], and tabs are shown as [Tab].

Code placement

WordPerfect automatically places codes in a logical order. Codes that affect the entire document will be placed first, followed by codes that affect pages, paragraphs, lines, and finally, characters. WordPerfect deletes duplicate or redundant codes.

Inserting the Date

We use dates in letters and many other documents. You can have WordPerfect insert the correct date automatically in two different ways. When you insert the date as *text*, today's date is inserted into the document just as if you typed it yourself. That date will appear no matter when you open or print the document.

When you insert the date as a *code*, today's date will be inserted just as if you had entered it as text, but it will automatically change if you open or print the document some other day. So, if you start a letter on one day and include the date as code, then complete and print the letter on another day, the printed copy will show the date that you printed the letter.

To insert the date:

1. Select Tools ➤ Date (or press Shift+F5) to see the options Text, Code, and Format. If you select Tools ➤ Date, you'll see a small menu; if you press Shift+F5, you'll see the Date dialog box, as shown in the figure.

2. Select Text to insert the current date as text, or select Code to insert the date as a code.

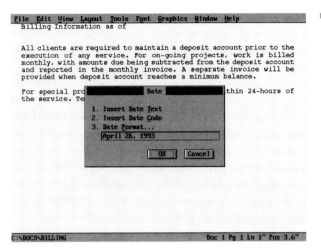

■ *The Date dialog box*

Read what you need

  Using the date code

Do not use the date code function if you want a reminder when the letter was originally written or mailed. When you later open the document the current date will appear.

  Erasing the date code

When you enter the date as a code, the date appears on screen, but it is stored as a single code in the document. To erase the date, you only need to press Del or Backspace once, as if you were deleting a single character.

  Easy dates

The Date Text and Date Code commands are available on the Tools button bar.

Changing Date Formats

WordPerfect's default date format is the one you'll probably use most often. However, WordPerfect provides twelve common date formats to choose from. You can also create your own custom date formats. For more information, see "Creating Custom Date Formats" later in this lesson.

To select a different date format:

1. Select Tools ➤ Date ➤ Format to display a dialog box listing common date formats, as shown in the figure.

2. Select one of the formats.

3. Click on OK.

4. Insert the date as text or code.

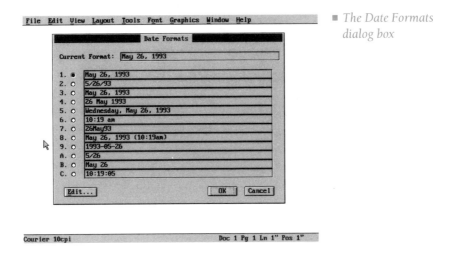

*■ The Date Formats
dialog box*

 Formatting existing dates

Dates entered as a code following the insertion point will change automatically to conform to the new date format. To change dates already
inserted, place the insertion point at the start of the document before selecting a new format. Dates entered as text will not be affected.

 A personal log

Select a date format that contains both the date and time, then use it to
record your activities, log phone calls, or maintain accounts for billing
purposes.

 Button bar

 The Date Format command is available from the Tools button bar.

Creating Custom Date Formats

If you do not like any of the date formats provided by WordPerfect, you can create your own. You can include roman numerals in dates and even add the seconds to times.

The custom format is stored as a code with the active document, so it is only available for that document.

To create your own date format:

1. Select Tools ➤ Date ➤ Format ➤ Edit to display the dialog box shown in the figure. The box shows the makeup of the current format in an Edit text box, a list of date codes, and a list of time codes.

2. Select the desired codes from the date and time lists. Double-click on the code or highlight the code and select Insert. The code will appear in brackets in the Edit box.

3. Add any desired spacing, punctuation, or text in the Edit box. A sample of the formatted date will appear in the dialog box as you select and edit options.

4. Click on OK.

5. Select Tools ➤ Date, then Text or Code, to insert the date into your document.

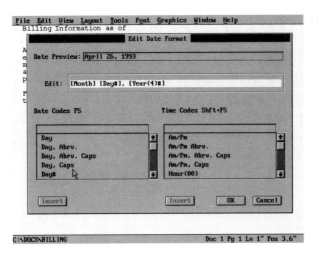

■ *The Edit Date Format dialog box*

TIP   **Some sample custom formats**

Use these examples to help create custom formats:

Codes	Result
[Day], [Month] [Day#], [Year(4)#]	Sunday, June 12, 1993
[Hour(24)#]:[Minute#]:[Seconds#]	13:12:34
[Year(4), Roman#]	MCMXCIII
Day [Day#] of [Month] in [Year(4)#]	Day 12 of June in 1993

TIP   **Select a base format**

To speed up the process of creating of custom format, select the format in the Date Format dialog box that most closely resembles the custom format desired, then select Edit.

Repeating Keystrokes

Sometimes you'll want to repeat a certain keystroke a specific number of times. For example, you may want to place a dotted line across the screen or move the insertion point a specific number of spaces. You also might need to repeat a certain command more than once—to delete the next five words or seven lines, for instance.

You can use the Repeat command to perform repeated actions easily and quickly.

To repeat characters or commands:

1. Select Edit ➤ Repeat (or press Ctrl+R) to display the Repeat dialog box, as shown in the figure. The default value of 8 indicates that the next nonnumeric keystroke will be entered eight times.

2. If you want a different number of repetitions, type a new number.

3. While the Repeat dialog box is displayed, type the keystroke or press the command to be repeated. You can repeat any single character or one keyboard command.

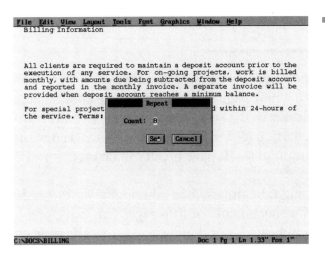

The Repeat dialog box

Printing dashed lines

To print a line of dashes across the screen, select Edit ➤ Repeat, type **67**, then press -. The repetition number depends on your font and size.

Using Repeat to delete

To quickly delete the next ten words, press Ctrl+R, type **10**, then press Ctrl+Backspace. To delete five lines, place the cursor at the start of the first line, press Ctrl+R, type **5**, then press Ctrl+End.

Changing the default repeat

To change the default number of repetitions, press Ctrl+R, type the new repeat number, press Enter, then select Set.

Read what you need

Inserting Page Breaks

As you type, WordPerfect will divide your document into pages automatically. When a new page starts, a single line appears across the screen and the Pg indicator in the status bar increases by one. Automatic page breaks are called *soft page breaks,* and they are marked with the [SPg] codes. The position of a soft page break can change as you insert or delete text.

But there might be times when you might want to end a page yourself, such as for a short memo or title page. This calls for a *hard page break,* which is indicated by a double line across the page and the [HPg] code.

To insert a page break:

—   Press Ctrl+Enter, or select Layout ➤ Alignment ➤ Hard Page.

WordPerfect will insert a double line like the ones shown in the figure.

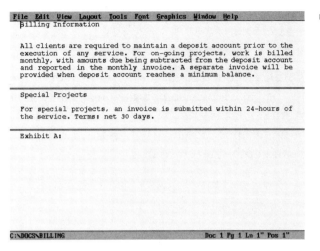

■ *A document showing two hard page breaks*

Beware of redundant page breaks

If you add enough text above a hard page break, WordPerfect may insert a soft page break when the page becomes full. When you print the document, a blank page will be printed—between the soft and hard page breaks. Before printing a document, scroll through it to check the position of page breaks.

Deleting hard page breaks

To delete a hard page break, place the insertion point just above the page break line and press Del, or place the insertion point just after the page break line and press Backspace.

Do not paginate with blank lines

Use hard page breaks when you want to end a page; do not press Enter until WordPerfect breaks pages for you. The blank lines make it more time-consuming to scroll through a document, and they will create havoc if you later add text to the page.

Preventing Widow and Orphan Lines

Because WordPerfect divides pages by simply counting lines, without considering how the page looks, some page breaks may divide paragraphs inappropriately. An *orphan* is a single line that is printed on the top of a page. A *widow* is a line appearing by itself on the bottom of a page. Both are unattractive, and both can be avoided.

To eliminate widow and orphan lines:

1. Place the insertion point at the beginning of the document.
2. Select Layout ➤ Other to display the Other Format dialog box.
3. Select Widow/Orphan Protect.
4. Click on OK.

When changing pages, WordPerfect will now shift lines up or down, sometimes printing fewer than the set number of lines per page, to avoid widow and orphan lines.

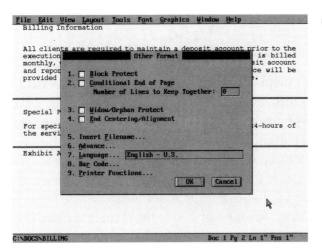

■ *The Other Format dialog box*

Position the insertion point

When you select Widow/Orphan Protect, WordPerfect inserts a code at the beginning of the current page. To protect the entire document, press Home, Home, ↑ before selecting Widow/Orphan Protect.

Removing protection

To remove widow/orphan protection from the current page, delete the [Wid\Orph: On] code on that page. To turn protection off for subsequent pages, place the insertion point on the page, select Layout ➤ Other, then select Widow/Orphan Protect.

Check page breaks yourself

Widow/Orphan Protect only prevents a paragraph from being broken incorrectly. It will not, for example, prevent a title or subtitle from printing on the last line of a page. So even with Widow/Orphan Protect active, you should scan important documents for proper page breaks before printing.

Read what you need

Changing the Display Magnification

The default display magnification of your WordPerfect documents is set at Margin Width. This means that characters will be enlarged or reduced so the page fits across the full width of the screen.

If you are in graphics or page views, you can change the magnification to display a full page or more on screen at one time, or to enlarge the text to make it easier to read. For example, when you set magnification at 100%, the text and graphics appear about the same size on screen as they do on the printed page. When set at 200%, the display is twice the printed size.

You can edit and format your document no matter what magnification you select.

To change the magnification:

1. Select View ➤ Zoom.

2. Select a percentage. The options are 50%, 75%, 100%, 125%, 150%, 200%, 300%, Margin Width, Page Width, and Full Page.

The figure shows a document in 75% magnification.

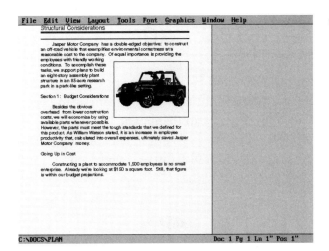

■ *A document in 75% magnification*

 Working in enlarged display

If the line length is wider than the page, display the horizontal scroll bar to make scrolling easier.

 Ribbon

 To select Zoom options from the ribbon, pull down the first list box on the left.

 Margin Width versus Page Width

Both Margin Width and Page Width adjust the magnification to fill the screen while displaying the full line length. In Page Width, however, the text is reduced slightly to display the right and left margins of the page.

Previewing the Printed Page

You can display a detailed facsimile of your printed document using Print Preview. While you cannot edit the document in preview mode, as in graphics or page views, you can display facing pages, as they would appear bound in a book, or zoom in to enlarge a specific portion of text.

You can preview a document from any view—text, graphics, or page.

To preview your document:

— Select File ➤ Print Preview (or press Shift+F7, 7).

To exit from preview:

— Select File ➤ Close (or press F7) or click on the Close button.

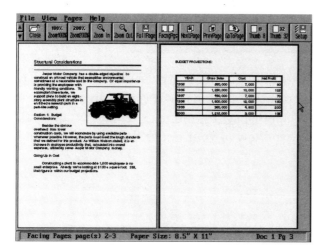

■ *Print Preview showing facing pages*

More Print Preview options

Enhanced options and thumbnail previews are new to version 6.0.

Button bar

Click on the Preview button to display the Print Preview.

Graphics view versus Print Preview

Print Preview will provide a more accurate view of the printed document than graphics view can, and it allows you to display multiple pages at one time for an overall view. However, you cannot edit or format the document in Print Preview.

Read what you need

Using Print Preview Options

Even if you work in graphics or page views, it pays to preview your document before printing it. Preview is especially useful with long documents, since you can display thumbnail sketches of up to 255 pages at one time. For an overview of your entire document, nothing beats Print Preview.

To use Print Preview options:

1. Select File ➤ Print Preview. The Print Preview status bar reports the zoom scale, paper size, document number, and the number of the displayed page.

2. Change the display as desired:

   — Press PgUp and PgDn to display other document pages.

   — Use the View menu and button bar to change the magnification, zoom specific portions into view, and change the number of pages displayed.

   — When a single page is displayed, you can enlarge a specific area up to 1000% by dragging the mouse pointer over the section on the previewed page.

   — Use the Pages menu to display other document pages.

The figure shows an eight-page thumbnail sketch.

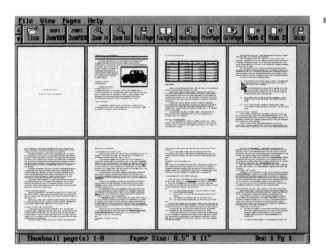

■ *An eight-page thumbnail section*

Thumbnails

Select the Thumb 8 or Thumb 32 buttons to display a thumbnail sketch of multiple pages. Select View ➤ Thumbnails to select from 1, 2, 4, 8, 32, or Other. Select Other to specify the number of pages, up to 255.

Zooming the Preview page

When you zoom in to enlarge the page, WordPerfect displays horizontal and vertical scroll bars. Use the scroll bars or other cursor-movement keys to scroll the image.

It's So Easy...   See Page...

Lesson 7

Working with Multiple Documents and Windows

Y ou can open and work on up to nine different documents at the same time in WordPerfect. This can be a great convenience if, say, you're typing a report and you need to refer back to a document you typed last week. Instead of looking for a printout of the document, you can open it in its own window and refer to it while you are typing your current report. Or you could outline a document in one window and write it in another, referring back to your outline as needed.

You can also use windows to copy or move text from one document to another, just as easily as you can move text from one location to another in the same document. In this lesson, you'll learn how to take best advantage of these new WordPerfect 6 features.

Opening Multiple Documents

Working with multiple documents can vastly increase your productivity and efficiency. You can write or edit one document while using others for reference. When you open a second document, the one originally displayed is not erased, it is just moved into the background.

To open another document:

— When one document is on the screen, select File ➤ Open or File ➤ File Manager to open another.

— Select File ➤ New to open a blank document window. You can then type a new document or open another document to be placed in the blank window.

To open several documents at one time:

1. Select File ➤ File Manager.

2. Select OK to accept the default directory or type in the complete path of another directory, including its drive letter. A directory of the disk will appear on the screen.

3. Highlight the name of each document you want to open and press the spacebar to select it.

4. Select Open into New Document or press Enter. A dialog box appears asking you to confirm that you want to open all of the marked documents.

5. Select Yes.

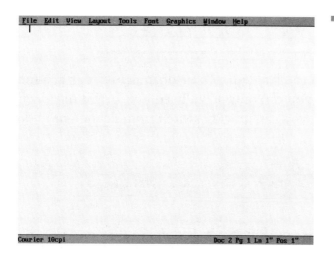

■ *A second document window. Notice that the status bar indicator reads "Doc 2."*

Read what you need

 Where did that document come from?

If you select File ➤ New, and then perform any editing or formatting in the blank screen before opening another document, the new document will open yet another window.

 Combining documents

To insert the text of a file on disk into the displayed document, use File ➤ Retrieve.

 Watch those windows

Depending on your computer system, opening multiple documents may slow WordPerfect's response to keystrokes and editing. Avoid opening unnecessary documents.

Switching between Documents

While you can have up to nine documents open at a time, only one is active. That is, you can only actually edit or format one document at a time. However, you can quickly switch from document to document.

To switch between documents:

1. Select Window ➤ Switch To (or press F3) to display a list of open documents like the one in the figure.

2. Click on the document you wish to edit, view, print, or save.

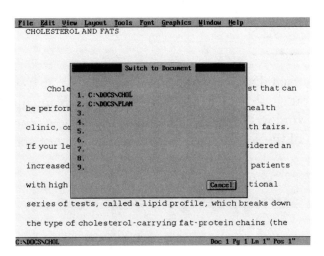

■ *The Switch To Document list*

Read what you need

 TIP   ### One view, mixed magnification

Changing views (from text to graphics, for example) in one document will affect the views of the other documents. Changing the magnification of one document will not affect another.

 TIP   ### Moving back and forth

Select Window ➤ Next or Window ➤ Previous to move from document to document. You can also select Window ➤ Switch (Shift+F3) to switch between the last two recently used documents.

 TIP   ### Prying eyes?

If you have a document whose contents you'd rather not share with others in your office, try this trick. Select File ➤ New to open a blank window. Press Shift+F3 to return to your document and continue working. If someone who should not see your work approaches, press Shift+F3 to display the blank window.

Creating Windows

By default, each document appears *maximized*, so that it fills the entire screen. If you would like to see more than one document at a time, you can create windows for your documents. A window represents a smaller portion of the screen that you can resize or move about.

To place a document in a window:

— Select Window ➤ Frame.

To place a document in the smallest possible window:

— Select Window ➤ Minimize. The window will be about the size of the one in the figure.

To remove a window and return the document to full size:

— Select Window ➤ Maximize.

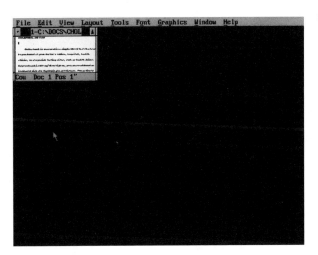

■ *A minimized window*

 Windows with a view

You can display windows in text, graphics, and page views. Windows in text view are less visually pleasing but provide the same capabilities as those in graphics or page views.

 Working with windows

The top border of a window's frame is called the title bar. The ▲ on the far right of the title bar is the *maximize* button. Click on this button to re-move the frame and make the window full size. The ▼ on the title bar is the *minimize* button. Click on this to reduce the window to its smallest possible size. The square on the left side of the title bar is the *exit box*. Click on this for the option to exit the document. The title bar also dis-plays the name of the document.

Displaying Multiple Windows

If you are working on several complex documents, you can move and copy text between them more efficiently if you display all of them on the screen. You can divide the screen into as many as nine windows at one time and move from window to window using the mouse or keyboard.

There are two ways to display multiple windows. When you *tile* windows, your documents appear in separate non-overlapping windows. When you *cascade* windows, the windows are stacked on one another. The top window occupies most of the screen, but you can still see the title bars of other open windows.

To tile windows:

— Select Window ➤ Tile.

To cascade windows:

— Select Window ➤ Cascade. The figure shows two cascaded windows.

To switch between displayed windows:

— Click on the window you want to make active. You can also change windows using Shift+F3 and the Window menu options.

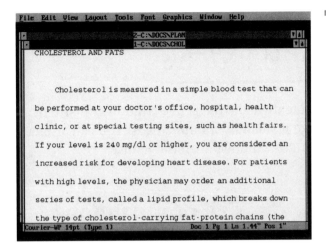

■ *Cascaded windows*

Read what you need

 Overlapping windows

When windows overlap, making one active will bring it into the foreground.

 Working with windows

Each window has its own title and status bar, but only one menu bar, ribbon, and button bar will appear. The settings in the ribbon will change to reflect those in the active window. Menu bar selections, such Save and Print, work on the active document.

 Telling active from inactive

Only one document window can be active at a time. In graphics view, the title bars of inactive windows are grayed. In text mode, the inactive windows have single-line borders and the active window has double-line borders.

Changing the Size and Position of Windows

You can quickly make the active window full-size by maximizing it, or you can make it small by minimizing it. You can also customize the size and position of windows with the mouse.

To change the size of a window:

— Drag one of the corners to change both the height and width of a window at the same time.

— Drag the left or right border to change the width.

— Drag the bottom border to change the height.

When you make a window narrower than the full screen width, the default Margin Width magnification will automatically result in a reduced character size. You may not be able to read the text in a small window unless you change the magnification to 100% or greater.

To move a window:

— Click on the top border and drag the mouse in the direction you want to move the window.

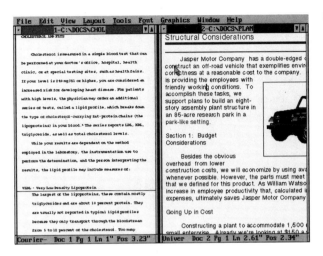

■ *Windows moved side-by-side, with one window in the default Margin Width view, the other enlarged to 100%*

Getting the correct size and position

As you drag the mouse, an outline of the window moves along with it. When the outline is the size you want or in the correct position, release the mouse button. You cannot move a window beyond the edge of the screen.

Minimized means smallest

You cannot reduce the size of a minimized window.

Read what you need

Moving Text between Documents

You can move and copy text from one open document to another, whether or not both documents are displayed at the same time. The technique is similar to that for moving text within a document.

To move or copy text between documents:

1. Switch to the document containing the text you want to move.

2. Select the text you want to move or copy. The figure shows a selected block of text.

3. Select Edit ➤ Cut and Paste to move text, deleting it from its original document; or select Edit ➤ Copy and Paste to insert a duplicate of the text in another document.

4. Switch to the document you want to place the text in, or select File ➤ New to insert it into a new document.

5. Press Enter or select Edit ➤ Paste.

File Edit View Layout Tools Font Graphics Window Help			
1—C:\DOCS\PLAN			
1995	560,000	7,000	80
1996	1,250,000	10,000	125
1997	490,000	7,000	70
1998	1,800,000	12,000	150
1999	960,000	4,800	200
2000	1,215,000	9,000	135

Block on   Doc 1 Pg 2 Ln 4.26" Pos 1"

2—(Untitled)

Courier 10cpi   Doc 2 Pg 1 Ln 1" Pos 1"

■ *Text about to copied
from one document to
another*

 FOR MORE...   ### Using the Move dialog box

You can also use the Move dialog box (press Ctrl+F4) to cut and copy text. Refer to Lesson 5 for more information about moving and copying text.

 TIP   ### Be prepared

Before selecting the text, prepare a location for it in the target document. At a minimum, place the insertion point where you want the text to be inserted.

 TIP   ### Moving text to unopened documents

You can move and copy text from a open document to one not yet opened. Select the text you want to cut or copy, then select Edit ➤ Cut and Paste or Edit ➤ Copy and Paste. Open the other document, then press Enter or select Edit ➤ Paste. Before opening the second document, you can close the first.

Exiting Multiple Documents

When you have two or more modified documents open, you can save each individually or save them all at once when you exit WordPerfect. Save individual documents just as you learned to in Lesson 2.

To exit WordPerfect from multiple documents:

1. Select File ➤ Exit WP. You will see a dialog box similar to that in the figure.

2. Select Save and Exit to save all of the documents that have been modified.

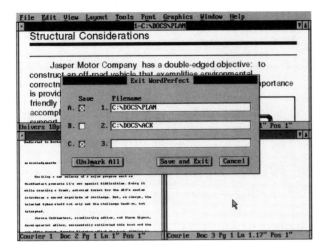

■ *The Exit WordPerfect dialog box showing modified, unchanged, and new documents*

Don't forget to save them all

Saving one document individually will not affect (save) a modified document in the inactive window.

Saving new documents

When you select Save and Exit, you will prompted to enter names for any yet unnamed documents.

Changing your mind

To skip saving a modified document, delete the X next to document's name in the Exit WordPerfect dialog box. Just be careful—any changes you've made to the document will be lost.

Let's Do It!

You now know how easy it is to edit a document using WordPerfect. Let's practice your new editing skills.

Opening Documents

We'll start by creating and saving a small document. Then, we'll practice opening the document using the Open dialog box and File Manager.

1. Start WordPerfect.

2. Type the following text:

```
Cholesterol is measured in a simple blood test
that can be performed at your doctor's office,
hospital, health clinic, or at special testing
sites, such as health fairs. If you level is 240
mg/dl or higher, you are considered an increased
risk for developing heart disease.
```

3. Select File ➤ Save (or press Ctrl+F12), type **CHOL**, and click on OK.

4. Select File ➤ Close to clear the window.

Now let's practice opening the document.

5. Select File ➤ Open.

6. Type **CHOL**, then click on OK. When you open a document, the insertion point is automatically at the top of the page.

7. Select File ➤ Close to clear the window.

Now let's use File Manager to open the CHOL document.

8. Select File ➤ File Manager and click on OK. A list of files in the default directory appears.

9. Scroll the list to highlight CHOL, then press Enter to accept Open into New Document, the default setting.

10. Select File ➤ Close to clear the window.

11. Select File ➤ Exit WP ➤ Exit if you're not ready to go on.

Inserting, Selecting, and Editing Text

Now let's add some text to the document; then we'll practice selecting text and using the Undo and Undelete commands.

1. Open the document named CHOL if it is not already on your screen.

2. Place the insertion point at the end of the last sentence in the document.

3. Press Enter twice to insert a blank line.

4. Press Tab to indent the paragraph, then type the following:

    ```
    For patients with high levels, the physician may
    order an additional series of tests, called a
    lipid profile, which breaks down the type of
    cholesterol-carrying fat-protein chains (the
    lipoproteins) in your blood. The series reports
    LDL, HDL, triglyceride, as well as total
    cholesterol levels.
    ```

5. Place the insertion point in front of the first paragraph.

6. Hold down the left mouse button, then drag the mouse to the end of the paragraph. If you're not using the mouse, position the insertion point, select Edit ➤ Block, then use the ↓ and → keys to select the text.

7. Press Del. Oops! We really don't want to delete all that text.

8. Select Edit ➤ Undelete (or press Esc) to display the Undelete dialog box.

9. Select Restore.

10. Place the insertion point before the period at the end of the first paragraph.

11. Press the spacebar to insert a space.

12. Type (**and possibly death!**). Well, that may be a little too morbid.

13. Select Edit ➤ Undo (or press Ctrl+Z) to delete the text.

14. Select File ➤ Save. Since the document already has a name, it is saved immediately.

15. Select File ➤ Exit WP ➤ Exit if you're not ready to go on.

Moving and Copying Text

Next we'll move and copy text and save a section of text as a separate document. We'll start by copying some text to make a title.

1. Open the document named CHOL if it is not already on your screen.

2. Place the insertion point at the start of the document.

3. Press Enter twice to insert two blank lines.

4. Select the word *Cholesterol* in the first paragraph.

5. Place the mouse pointer on the selected word, hold down the left mouse button (do not release it until after the next step), then drag the pointer to the top of the document, in the first blank line.

6. Hold down the Ctrl key, release the mouse button, then release the Ctrl key.

If you don't have a mouse, you can perform the same action by selecting the text and selecting Edit ➤ Copy and Paste. Then move the insertion point to the top of the document and select Edit ➤ Paste.

Now we'll save a portion of the text as a separate document.

7. Select the entire first paragraph.

8. Select File ➤ Save As.

9. Type **INTRO**, then click OK to save the text.

10. Select File ➤ Save.

11. Select File ➤ Exit WP ➤ Exit if you're not ready to go on.

Some Advanced Editing

Let's add the date to the document named CHOL, quickly insert a line across the screen, then see how it looks enlarged and reduced.

1. Open the document named CHOL if it is not already on your screen.

2. Place the insertion point at the start of the document.

3. Press Enter twice to insert a blank line.

4. Move the insertion point to the top of the document, at the left margin in the blank line.

5. Select Tools ➤ Date ➤ Code to insert the date as a code.

6. Move the insertion point in the blank line below the date.

7. Press Ctrl+R to display the Repeat dialog box.

8. Type **65**, then press the hyphen (-) to draw the line. Now we'll take a look at your document in a different perspective.

---

9. Select View ➤ Zoom ➤ 200% to enlarge the document.

10. Select View ➤ Zoom ➤ 50% to reduce it.

11. Select View ➤ Zoom ➤ Margin Width to return to the default display.

12. Select File ➤ Print Preview.

13. Select the File ➤ Close (or press F7).

14. Select File ➤ Save.

15. Select File ➤ Exit WP ➤ Exit if you're not ready to go on.

Working with Windows

Finally, we'll see how to work with more than one document.

1. Open the document named CHOL if it is not already on your screen.

2. Select the last paragraph in the document.

3. Select Edit ➤ Copy and Paste.

4. Select File ➤ New to start a new document.

5. Select Edit ➤ Paste to insert the text you copied.

6. Select Window ➤ Tile to display both windows on the screen. Your screen will look like Figure 2.1.

7. Select Window ➤ Minimize to make the active window the minimum size.

8. Click anywhere on the other window to select it (or press Shift+F3).

9. Click on its maximize button or select Window ➤ Maximize to maximize this window.

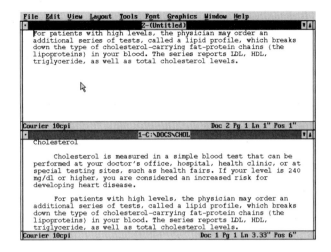

■ FIGURE 2.1:
Tiled windows with copied text

10. Select Window ➤ Switch (or press Shift+F3). The other document is still in its minimized window.

Now exit WordPerfect without saving either document.

11. Select File ➤ Exit WP.

12. Click on (Un)mark All.

13. Click on Exit.

PART

3

Formatting Your Documents

What's the difference between a laser printer and a typewriter? Your imagination. With a typewriter you're pretty much restricted to one or two sizes and styles of characters. With WordPerfect's formatting features and a good printer, the appearance of your documents is limited only by your imagination.

We'd all like to think that our words are golden, that they are read because of what we have to say. But let's face the truth—it's a fickle world out there. That's why cosmetics are a billion-dollar business. Looking good is half the battle.

In these lessons, you'll learn how to format your documents so that they're instantly eye-catching.

It's So Easy...   See Page...

Lesson 8

Changing the Appearance of Characters

You can use WordPerfect's formatting features to achieve a variety of effects. With a judicious use of fonts, sizes, and format styles, you can even give your documents a desktop-published, professional look—but don't overdo it! Too many fonts and styles make text more difficult to read and unpleasing to the eye.

Using Bold, Underline, and Other Formats

Using the Font menu, you can easily format characters as boldface, underline, double underline, italics, outline, shadow, small caps, redline, and strikeout. The screen on the facing page shows all of these formats.

■ To format characters:

1. Type until you are ready to format characters.

2. Pull down the Font menu and select the desired style.

— Select Font ➤ Bold (or press F6) to boldface.

— Select Font ➤ Underline (or press F8) to underline.

— Select Font ➤ Italics (or press Ctrl+I) to italicize.

To format in two styles, such as bold and italic, select both formats.

3. Type the characters.

4. Pull down the Font menu and select the style again to turn it off, or select Font ➤ Normal (or press Ctrl+N) to turn off all character formats.

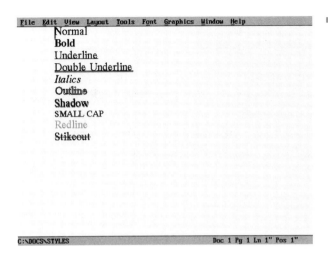

Oops! **My entire document is underlined!**

You can end up with some weird formatting if you forget to turn off a style after typing the characters you wanted to format. To remove formats, see "Changing Formats" later in this section.

TIP **But it doesn't look italic!**

In text view, formatted characters appear in a different color. In graphics view, they appear as they will be printed. Your printer may not be capable of printing all character formats in every format.

FOR MORE... **Changing your mind**

To change the appearance of text after typing it, you can select the text and then apply boldface, italic, or any other style. For more information on selecting text, see Lesson 4.

Changing Type Fonts and Sizes

A *font* is a group of characters in a particular size and style. To some extent, the fonts and sizes you can use in your documents depend on your printer's capabilities. WordPerfect comes with several fonts that you can use, even if they are not built into your printer. And you can purchase additional fonts from a variety of suppliers.

To change the font or font size:

1. Select Font ➤ Font (or press Ctrl+F8) to display the Font dialog box, as shown in the figure.

2. Pull down the Font list box to display available fonts.

3. Select a font from the list.

4. Pull down the Size list box to display available sizes.

5. Select the size.

6. Select other font attributes.

7. Click on OK.

8. Type the text you want in that font and size.

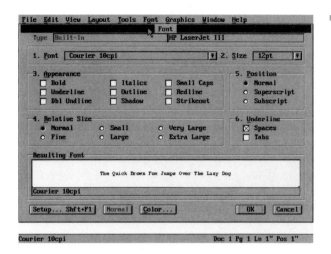

■ *The Font dialog box*

 TIP   ## Changing the font of existing text

To change the font of text you've already typed, select the text first, then select options from the Font dialog box or ribbon. To enter a portion of text in a new font, type the text first, select it, then choose the font.

 TIP   ## Multiple formats

If you are using multiple formats, use the Font dialog box, rather than the Font menu, to select a number of styles (such as bold and underline) at one time. This eliminates the need to pull down the menu for each style.

 BUTTON BAR   ## Easy font changes

 You can click on the Font button to display the Font button bar.

 RIBBON   ## Another way to save time

 To change fonts using the ribbon, pull down the Font list to select a font and the Size list to select a size. The Font and Size boxes will indicate the font of the text at the insertion point.

Changing Relative Font Size

Normally, to select a font size, you will use the Font dialog box or the ribbon. However, there may be times when you'll want to use a special WordPerfect feature that permits you to change the size of characters *relative* to the current font. This size is expressed as a percentage of the current font, as shown in the figure.

To select a relative font size:

1. Select Font ➤ Size/Position.

2. Select the size: Normal Size, Fine, Small, Large, Very Large, Extra Large, Normal Position, Superscript, Subscript.

3. Type the text.

4. Select Font ➤ Size/Position ➤ Normal Size to change back to the normal size.

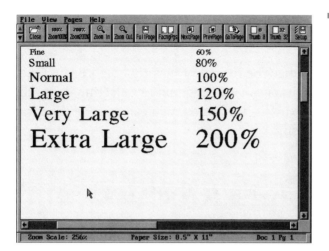

■ *Percentages used for relative font sizes*

To save time

Use relative sizes when you want to quickly change the size but not the font of text.

When it doesn't look correct

If the selected sizes do not appear when printed, they may not be available on your printer. In some cases, WordPerfect will automatically select an alternate font or size for you.

How relative sizes work

The size of the relative font depends on the current font being used. For example, if the current font is a 12-point font and you select Large, the resulting font will be 14.4-point, and if the current font is 18-point, the resulting font is 21.6. Fonts are measured in points, and there are about 72 points to an inch.

Changing Formats

You can change the format of new text before you type it, or you can change the appearance of existing text by selecting it and then applying the format. Once text is formatted, you can remove the format or add other formats easily.

■ To remove formats from text:

— Reveal codes and delete the format code preceding the text, or select the formatted text, then pull down the Font menu and select the format you want to remove.

■ To add additional formats:

— Select the text and choose a format from the Font menu, Font dialog box, or ribbon. The figure shows the appearance of the Font menu with two formats selected.

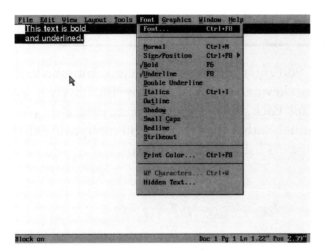

I can't turn it off!

If you can't turn off a style, you may have selected too much text. If you
select normal as well as formatted text, the style of the formatted text will
not be checked in the Font menu. Selecting the style again will apply the
format to all of the highlighted text, not remove it.

Turning off styles and fonts

Selecting Font ➤ Normal cancels *styles* selected from the Font menu and
dialog box, but it does not cancel *fonts* and *sizes* selected from the dialog
box or ribbon.

Removing styles

You can use the Search and Replace dialog box to quickly remove styles
from text. Just press the appropriate key (F6 for bold, for example) while
you're in the Search For box, and leave <Nothing> in the Replace With
box. *Warning:* You cannot replace styles alone using the Replace command.

Read
what
you
need

Changing the Case of Characters

Normally, you enter uppercase characters from the keyboard by pressing the Shift key or the Caps Lock key. But have you every accidentally pressed Caps Lock, only to notice the mistake after you've typed several paragraphs? Rather than retype, you can quickly change the case of existing characters using the Edit menu.

To change the case of text:

1. Select the text you want to change.

2. Select Edit ➤ Convert Case (or press Shift+F3).

3. Select Upper, Lower, or Initial Caps.

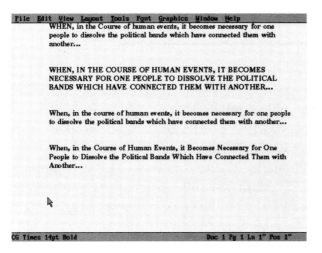

■ *Text in original and converted cases*

 Initial caps

The Initial Caps option changes the first letter of every word (except for articles like *a* and *the* and prepositions like *for* and *with*) to capital, not just the first letter of the sentence.

 That's not what I wanted

If you select Initial Caps by mistake, select the text, then select Lower. Only the first character of sentence will remain uppercase.

 Lowercase

Selecting lowercase will convert every character in a sentence except the first letter in the sentence and the pronoun *I*.

Inserting Special Characters

In this era of international business, it is no longer uncommon to find the need to print foreign-language characters, and mathematical, scientific, and graphic symbols.

WordPerfect has 15 character sets, numbered 0 to 14, that allow you to add thousands of special characters to your documents: ASCII (0), Multinational (1), Phonetic (2), Box Drawing (3), Typographic Symbols (4), Iconic Symbols (5), Math/Scientific (6), Math/Scientific Extended (7), Greek (8), Hebrew (9), Cyrillic (10), Japanese (11), User-Defined (12), Arabic (13), and Arabic Script (14). If your printer does not have the characters you want to use available internally, WordPerfect prints them as graphic images closely matching the font being used.

To insert special characters:

1. Select Font ➤ Characters (or press Ctrl+W) to see the WordPerfect Characters dialog box, as shown in the figure.

2. Pull down the Set list box and select the character set. The characters in that set are displayed in the Characters box.

3. Double-click on the character you want to insert, or select the character, then click on the Insert button.

The character will appear at the position of the insertion point, in a size to match that of the current font.

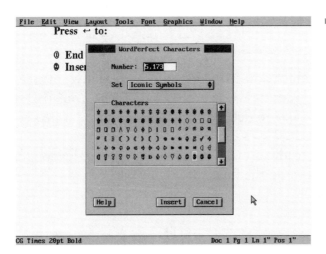

■ *The WordPerfect Characters dialog box with special characters in the background document*

Composing characters from the keyboard

Each character in a character set is associated with a number, starting with 0. If you know the set and number, you can use a special character without using the WordPerfect Characters dialog box. Just press Ctrl+A, type the set and number separated by a comma, and press Enter. For example, to use the → character, press Ctrl+A, type **6,21**, and press Enter to display the → character.

Instant characters

You can display some characters instantly by pressing Ctrl+A and typing the following: type ** to insert •, **co** to insert ©, **tm** to insert ™, **ro** to insert ®, **L-** to insert £, **Y=** to insert ¥, **/2** to insert ½, and **/4** to insert ¼. Check your manual for additional characters.

Characters and views

Use graphics view to insert characters. In text view, most of the characters will appear as small boxes, although they will print correctly.

Removing Redline and Strikeout

You use redline and strikeout to make tentative changes to a document, or when working with another individual. You strikeout text to show that you'd like to delete it, and you redline text that you'd like to add.

When are ready to make the final changes to the document, you can have WordPerfect do the final editing for you.

■ To remove redline and strikeout:

1. Select File ➤ Compare Documents ➤ Remove Markings. You'll see the Remove Markings dialog box, as shown in the figure.

2. Select Remove Redline Markings and Strikeout Text. Text that has been formatted as strikeout will be deleted, and the redline markings will be removed from text formatted with redline codes.

Select Remove Strikeout Text Only to leave redline markings on text.

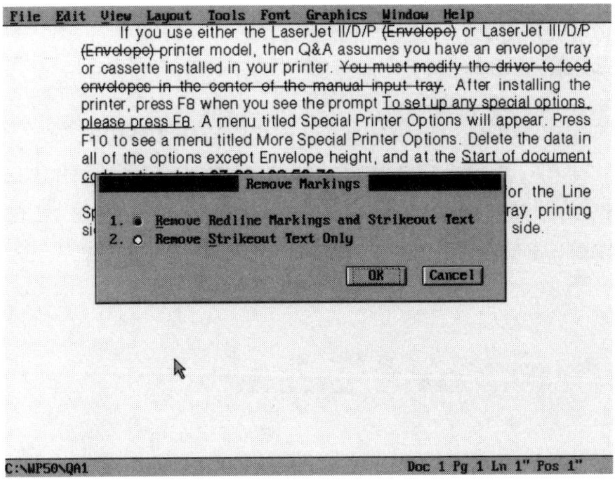

■ *Redline and Strikeout options*

Read what you need

TIP

Using redline and strikeout

When you want to add suggested text, format it as redline—select Font ➤ Redline. The text will appear on screen in a different color and print in reverse on a gray background. This informs other writers that the text is not part of the original document. When you feel some text should be deleted, format it as strikeout. Select the text, then choose Font ➤ Strikeout. The text will appear on screen in a different color and print with a line through it. This informs other writers that the text is part of the original document but that you feel it should be deleted.

If all of your suggestions are agreed upon, you can then use the Remove Redline Margins and Strikeout Text option.

TIP

Retaining strikeout text

If you choose not to delete some text formatted as strikeout, delete the strikeout codes ([StkOut On]) manually or by using the Search and Replace dialog box.

Using Hidden Text

Now you see it, now you don't. When you format text as *hidden*, you can choose whether or not it appears on screen and is printed with the document. Use hidden text to write reminders or notes that you want with the document but not printed with the final copy.

To format text as hidden:

1. Select Font ➤ Hidden Text to display the dialog box shown in the figure.
2. Select Hidden Text or press 1.
3. Click on OK.
4. Type the text you want to hide.
5. Select Font ➤ Hidden Text.
6. Select Hidden Text and click on OK.

To display hidden text:

1. Select Font ➤ Hidden Text.
2. Select Show All Hidden Text or press 2.
3. Click on OK.

To prevent hidden text from being printed, make sure the X does not appear in the Show All Hidden Text check box. If you forget to turn off the option, the text you wanted to hide will be printed.

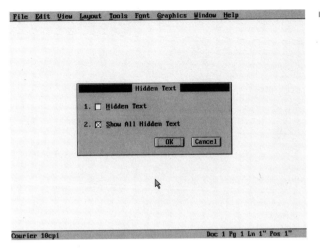

The Hidden Text dialog box

  Check Pagination Before Printing

Showing or hiding hidden text will affect the document's pagination. Before you print the document, set the Show All Hidden Text option as you want it to be for the printout, then scan the document for proper pagination.

  Converting Hidden Text

To remove the hidden text format from a section of text, first make sure that hidden text is displayed. Then, select Edit ➤ Reveal Codes and delete the [Hidden On] or [Hidden Off] code on either side of the text. When hidden text is not displayed, only the Hidden On code will appear in the Reveal Codes window—deleting the code will also delete the text itself.

Lesson 9

Formatting Lines

Attractive line formatting can make your document easier and more interesting to read. No matter how important your words, they have to be read to have any impact. By adjusting spacing and the alignment of text, you can help insure that your document has the maximum effect.

Changing Line Spacing

Line spacing changes the overall appearance of the document. It can be set for the entire document, or just for sections within it. Spacing is allowed in decimal increments, such as 1.5 or 2.3.

■ *To change line spacing:*

1. Place the insertion point where you want the new line spacing to take effect.

2. Select Layout ➤ Line to display the Line Format dialog box, as shown in the figure.

3. Select Line Spacing.

4. Enter the desired line spacing, or click on the up or down pointers to increase or decrease the spacing in one-tenth increments.

5. Click on OK.

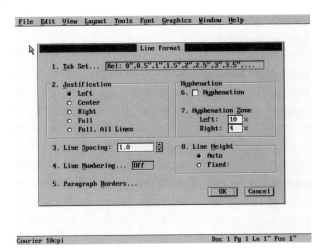

Position the insertion point

Line spacing affects the text from the insertion point down. To change the spacing of the entire document, press Home, Home, ↑ before changing the spacing. To change spacing of a portion of text, select the text first, then change the line spacing.

Avoid scrolling

Type your document single-spaced to reduce the amount of scrolling you'll have to do during the editing process. Then, before printing, change the line spacing where desired and make any adjustments.

Why doesn't it look correct?

In text view, text will appear on the screen in the nearest integer. For example, lines spaced at 1.5 will be double-spaced on the screen, although they will be printed at 1.5.

Read what you need

Centering Text

Titles and subtitles often look best when centered on the page. They provide a break in the text and call attention to a change in subject or purpose. You can center *single lines* or as many lines of existing text as you want.

To center a title or line of text:

1. Place the insertion point at the start of the line.

2. Select Layout ➤ Alignment to display alignment options, as shown in the figure.

3. Select Center. The cursor moves to the center of the screen.

4. Type the text you want centered.

5. Press Enter. Centering affects text up to the carriage return that ends the line.

6. To decenter centered text, reveal the codes and delete the [Cntr on Mar] or [Just:Center] code.

If you type more than one line, only the first will be centered.

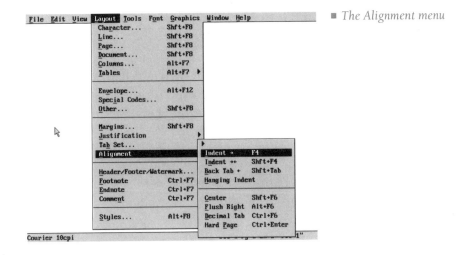

■ *The Alignment menu*

  To center existing text

To center a line of text, place the insertion point at the start of the line and select Layout ➤ Alignment ➤ Center (or press Shift+F7). To center a large section of text, select the text, then select Center from the ribbon or Justification menu.

  Using alternative methods

When you center text using Layout ➤ Justification ➤ Center, Layout ➤ Line ➤ Center, or the ribbon, centering does not end when you press Enter. To end the format, select Layout ➤ Justification ➤ Left, or select Left from the ribbon.

  Centering made simple

To center text using the ribbon, pull down the Justification box (showing Left by default) and select Center.

Aligning Text Flush Right

Flush right text is aligned on the right margin with an uneven margin on the left—just the opposite from regular unjustified text. This format is most commonly used in business announcements and programs.

To align a line of text on the right:

1. Select Layout ➤ Alignment ➤ Flush Right (or press Alt+F6). The cursor will move to the right margin.

2. Type the text. Characters entered will move to the left, and the [Flsh Rgt] code is inserted at the start of the text.

3. Press Enter.

4. To return flush right text to normal, use Reveal Codes and delete the [Flsh Rgt] or [Just:Right] codes.

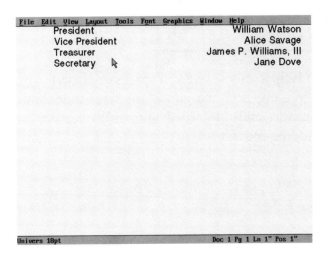

■ *Right-aligned text*

TIP   **Using the ribbon and the Justification menu**

You can also right-align text by selecting Layout ➤ Justification ➤ Right or by pulling down the Justification box on the ribbon and selecting Right. This affects text from the cursor position to the next justification code.

TIP   **To align existing text on the right**

Place the cursor *at the start* of the line, then select Layout ➤ Alignment ➤ Flush Right (or press Alt+F6). To right-align multiple lines, select them first, then use any method of right aligning.

TIP   **Combining left- and right-aligned text**

To format text as shown in the figure, type the text you want to appear at the left of the page, select Layout ➤ Alignment ➤ Flush Right (Alt+F6), then type the text aligned on the right. Just make sure the flush-right text does not collide with the characters on the left.

Creating Full Justification

When you fully justify text, extra spaces are inserted between words to align your text along both margins at the same time. You can select to justify lines that were ended by word wrap only, or every line of the paragraph, including the last.

To justify text:

1. Place the insertion point where you want justification to begin.

2. Select Layout ➤ Justification

3. Select Full or Full, All Lines. The figure shows both types of full justification.

4. To cancel justification, position the insertion point where you want to stop the justification, then select Layout ➤ Justification ➤ Left.

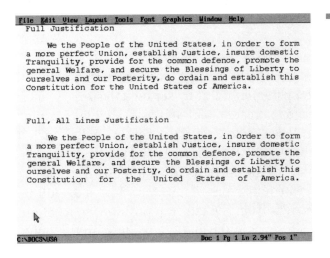

■ *Full and Full, All Lines justification*

Too many spaces!

Read what you need

As shown in the figure, unless the last line of the paragraph is nearly full, selecting Full, All Lines can result in unsightly spaces. There are also times when selecting Full justification will result in unsightly extra spaces. Hyphenation can alleviate this problem; see "Hyphenating Text Automatically" in Lesson 10 to learn more.

Justification in different views

In graphics and page views, the text will appear justified on the screen. In text view, text will not appear justified, but some words may shift up or down to indicate where lines will end when printed.

Easier justification

To justify text from the ribbon, pull down the Justification box and select Full.

Setting Tabs

Sometimes you might not use tabs for anything more than indenting the first line of a paragraph. But by setting tab stops, you can align columns on the page to create tables and lists, a table of contents, or forms.

By default, WordPerfect sets tab stops every half inch, but you can easily change these and set your own. The tab stops you set affect only the text from the start of the current paragraph down.

You can create four types of tab stop. With a default left tab, characters shift to the right from the tab stop position, so a column will be aligned on the left. A right tab aligns a column on the right by shifting characters to the left of the tab stop. Use a center tab to center text around the tab stop. A decimal tab aligns numbers on the decimal point.

To set tabs:

1. Select Layout ➤ Tab Set to display the Tab Set window, as shown in the figure.

2. Click on Clear All to delete all of the preset tabs. This makes it easy to reach those you set when typing.

3. Click at the position on the scale line—the ruler on top of the window—where you want to set the tab.

4. Click on the tab type: Left, Right, Center, or Decimal.

5. Optionally, click on Dot Leader.

6. Click on OK when done.

Text displayed in the window will automatically adjust to the tab stop position as you insert and delete tabs.

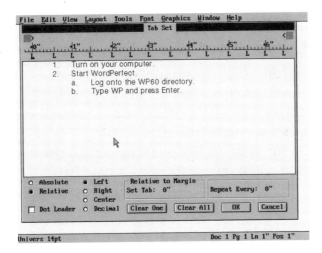

■ *The Tab Set window*

 Double-click to set a tab!

You can double-click at a position on the ruler to set a tab of the type already selected in the dialog box.

 To delete tabs

To delete a single tab, select the tab, then select Clear One or press Del. To return to the default tab setting, select Edit ➤ Reveal Codes and delete the [Tab Set] code.

 Relative versus absolute tabs

By default, WordPerfect uses relative tabs. If you set tabs, then change the left margin, the tabs will shift to maintain the same relative distance. So, if you set a tab at 2 inches, then increase the margins by one inch, the tab will shift to 3 inches. Click on Absolute in the Tab Set menu to set tabs that will not change as you change the margins.

Aligning Numbers on the Decimal Point

Use a *decimal tab* when you want to type a column of numbers. With a decimal tab, characters shift to the left as you type, until you enter a decimal point. Characters then move to the right. Numbers always look better when they are aligned at the decimal point.

If you plan your columns before typing, set a decimal tab in the Tab Set window. You can also set a decimal tab as you type.

To align numbers on the decimal point as you type:

1. Select Layout ➤ Alignment ➤ Decimal Tab (or press Ctrl+F6) until the insertion point is at the location where you want numbers to align.

2. Type the decimal number.

File	Edit	View	Layout	Tools	Font	Graphics	Window	Help

Left	Center	Right	Decimal
1.23	1.23	1.23	1.23
120.99	120.99	120.99	120.99
.98	.98	.98	.98

Univers 14pt   Doc 1 Pg 1 Ln 1.67" Pos 3.98"

■ *Numbers aligned using various tab types*

How decimal tabs work

Each time you select Decimal Tab (or press Ctrl+F6), the insertion point moves to the next tab stop on the right, but the tab is automatically changed for decimal alignment.

To align columns on the right as you type

If you want to create right-aligned text without setting a tab, press Ctrl+F6 to reach the right-aligned position, then type. The text will shift to the left. Press Enter or Tab when done.

Beware of colliding text!

Make sure your numbers do not collide with other text on the line.

It's So Easy...

Lesson 10

Formatting Paragraphs

The default paragraph format used by WordPerfect is the block style—every line, including the first one in a paragraph, starts at the left margin. In this lesson, you'll learn how to change the way paragraphs are arranged—by indenting them on the left or right, and by adding hyphens to even out lines on the right.

Indenting Paragraphs

If you want to indent the first line of a paragraph, just press the Tab key. But you might want to indent a whole paragraph from the left margin, or from both the right and left margins, as for a long quotation. You can create both styles easily with WordPerfect.

To indent a paragraph from the left margin:

1. Select Layout ➤ Alignment ➤ Indent → (or press F4).

2. Type the text.

3. Press Enter. The figure on the facing page shows several paragraphs indented from the left.

To indent a paragraph from both margins:

1. Select Layout ➤ Alignment ➤ Indent → ← (or press Shift+F4).

2. Type the text.

3. Press Enter.

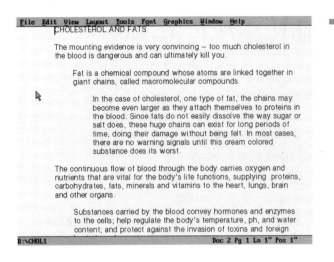

■ *Indented paragraphs*

TIP   ### How Indent works

Each time you select Indent, the left margin moves to the next tab stop to the right. Select Indent once to indent a paragraph a half inch (the first tab by default), twice for a one-inch indentation, and so on. Indent creates a temporary margin change. At the end of the line, WordPerfect moves the insertion point to the indented position, not the original margin, until you press Enter. You can use Indent to format existing paragraphs without affecting other text. Indent →← functions the same way but changes both the left and right margins.

 FOR MORE...   ### Indentations versus margins

You can indent a paragraph by changing the left margin. However, margin changes affect the entire document, so you'll have to reset the margin following the indented text if you do not want the margin change to affect the entire document. Change margins when you want the entire document, or a large portion of it, indented. See "Setting Margins" in Lesson 11 for more information.

Creating Hanging Indentation

Standard paragraphs have only the first line indented with remaining text flush on the left. *Hanging indentations* are just the opposite; the first line starts to the left of the rest of the paragraph. Use hanging indentations when you want paragraphs to stand out from each other, as with numbered paragraphs and outlines.

To create a numbered paragraph:

1. Select Layout ➤ Alignment ➤ Hanging Indent.
2. Type the paragraph number, followed by a period if desired.
3. Press Tab.
4. Type the text.
5. Press Enter to end the paragraph and return the insertion point to the left margin. The figure opposite shows an outline that uses numbered and lettered paragraphs.

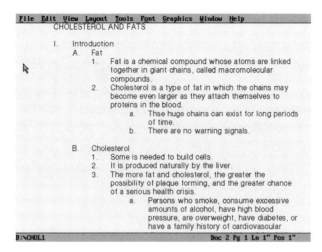

■ *An outline using hanging indentation*

 TIP **How hanging indentation works**

Hanging indentation actually inserts two codes, a left indentation and a backtab (margin release). The backtab moves the insertion point to the left margin of the first line. Subsequent lines start at the indent position until you press Enter.

 TIP **Hanging indentation from the keyboard**

To create numbered paragraphs without using the Layout menu, type the paragraph number, then press F4. WordPerfect will continue lines at the indented position. To create indented positions more to the right—for lower outline levels, for example—press Tab to reach the location where you want the paragraph number.

 TIP **Hanging text**

Hanging indentations can also be used for text. For this format, just select Layout ➤ Alignment ➤ Hanging Indent, then type the paragraph. To format this manually, press F4, then Shift+Tab, the backtab command.

Hyphenating Text Automatically

WordPerfect lets you type without pressing Enter at the end of each line. But at times, such as when long words are carried to the next line, a justified paragraph can have too many extra spaces between words.

Ordinary manual hyphenation slows down your typing by making you pause at the end of lines to make hyphenation decisions. When you use automatic hyphenation, however, WordPerfect actually divides words for you and adds hyphens at appropriate places.

To hyphenate automatically:

1. Place the insertion point where you want to begin hyphenation.

2. Select Layout ➤ Line.

3. Click on the Hyphenation option or press 6.

4. Click on OK.

5. WordPerfect will automatically insert a hyphen where appropriate. If WordPerfect's rules of hyphenation don't apply, a dialog box will appear asking you to confirm the hyphen position, as shown in the figure. Press the → and ← keys to move the hyphen to an appropriate place, then select Insert Hyphen.

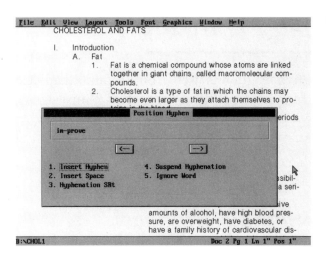

Hyphenating existing text

Turn on hyphenation either before you type or at the beginning of existing text. As you scroll through text, WordPerfect will hyphenate for you.

Deleting hyphens

To remove all of the automatic hyphenations, reveal codes and delete the [Hyphen: On] code at the beginning of the document. With words that are small enough to be combined on the next line, you can manually delete the [Auto Hyphen EOL] code to remove the hyphen. If you delete a [Soft Hyphen EOL] code, WordPerfect displays the Position Hyphen dialog box. Select Ignore Word or press 5 to delete the hyphen.

Read what you need

Entering Hyphens Yourself

Automatic hyphenation is useful, but it cannot handle every situation that calls for a hyphen character, such as minus signs in equations, or hyphenated words like son-in-law. WordPerfect offers hyphen characters for every occasion. The figure shows some text that contains several hyphens.

To create manual hyphens:

— Press the - key by itself in words that require hyphens, such as mother-in-law and son-in-law.

— Press Home, - to insert a minus sign for formulas, such as N=G−E.

— Press Ctrl+- (the Ctrl key and the - key together) to enter a "soft" hyphen when you want hyphenation to limit extra spaces.

— Press Home, Enter to insert an *invisible soft hyphen*, the [Hyph SRt] code.

— Press Ctrl+A, then type **m**- or - - to insert an em dash (—). Press Ctrl+A and type **n**- to insert an en dash (–).

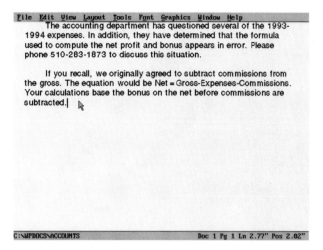

■ *Hyphenated text*

How WordPerfect divides words with manual hyphens

When you press - by itself, WordPerfect inserts a [-Hyphen] code. If you later add or delete text from the paragraph, WordPerfect will divide the word between lines at the hyphen. WordPerfect will not divide a formula at the position of the minus sign, entered with Home, -.

Soft hyphens—semi-automatic hyphenation

When you press Ctrl+-, no hyphen will appear on screen unless Word-Perfect needs to word-wrap the word between lines. If later editing forces the word to be wrapped, it will be hyphenated at that point even with hyphenation turned off. An invisible soft hyphen (Home, Enter) never appears on screen. WordPerfect will use that position to divide the word if later editing requires the word to be divided at the end of a line—but no hyphen will appear.

Lesson 11

Formatting Pages

Each time you start WordPerfect, standard settings are provided automatically to let you type and print documents without worrying about the size of the page. The default margins result in a page with 54 lines of text, with each line $6\frac{1}{2}$ inches wide. The text will appear neatly arranged when printed on standard business stationery, with text aligned on the left margin.

You don't have to change a thing if you like these settings and want to use them for every page of your document. But you can change any of these settings easily if you want other formats.

Setting the Margins

The page margins determine how much text will fit on each page. The right and left margins, for example, set the length of the printed line and can adjust for different widths of paper.

To make a document appear longer, make the margins a little wider. Make them smaller to fit as much text as possible on a page.

To set the margins:

1. Place the insertion point on the first line of the document.

2. Select Layout ➤ Margins (or press Shift+F8, M) to display the Margin Format dialog box, as shown in the figure.

3. Select Left Margin and type the margin setting.

4. Select Right Margin and type the margin setting.

5. Select Top Margin and enter the desired top margin.

6. Select Bottom Margin and enter the desired bottom margin.

7. Click on OK to close the dialog box.

8. To return a document to the default margins, reveal codes and delete the margin codes.

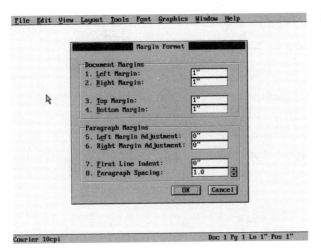

■ *The Margin Format dialog box*

Beware of your position!

When you change the left or right margins, WordPerfect inserts a code at the beginning of the paragraph in which the cursor is located. The change affects every paragraph from that position to the end of the document—or until the next margin size code. WordPerfect places the Top and Bottom margin code at the start of the page on which the cursor is located. So, place the insertion point on the first page you want to format.

Margins versus Indent

Use indents to change the margins of an individual paragraph or selection of text. Use margins to change the margins for the entire document.

Why did the margins change?

Some printers have minimum required margins. If you set smaller margins, WordPerfect automatically changes the settings to the printer's minimum.

Creating Title Pages

Title pages usually contain several lines of text centered both horizontally and vertically on the page. To get this effect, you could type the text, then set the top, left, and right margins so the text appears in the proper location. However, it's easier to take advantage of two WordPerfect functions that automatically center text between the top and bottom margins.

To create a title page:

1. Select Layout ➤ Page (or press Shift+F8, P) to display the Page Format dialog box, as shown in the figure.

2. Select Center Current Page.

3. Click on OK.

4. Type the text to be centered.

5. Press Ctrl+Enter to end the title page and start a new page.

The [Center Pg] code at the start of the page will automatically add the necessary blank lines to center the text between the top and bottom margins.

To center every document page from the insertion point to the end of the document:

— Select Layout ➤ Page ➤ Center Pages. WordPerfect inserts the [Cntr Pgs] code.

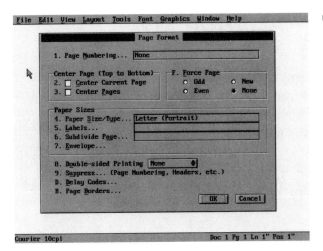

■ *The Page Format dialog box*

 TIP ### Text on center

The center page options only center text between the top and bottom margins—not between the left and right margins. To center text across the page, press Shift+F6 or select Layout ➤ Justification ➤ Center.

 TIP ### Watch those blank lines

If you want the text slightly higher than center, just add a few blank lines with the Enter key after typing the text. To print it slightly lower than center, add the lines above the text, but after the [Center Pg] code.

 TIP ### Canceling centered pages

To cancel centered pages, select Layout ➤ Page to display the Page Format menu, click on the option to turn it off, then click on OK. Alternatively, reveal codes, then delete the [Cntr Cur Pg:On] or [Cntr Pgs] code.

Selecting a Preset Page Size

Because many paper and envelope sizes are standard, you can change from one paper size to another without measuring and entering paper width and height yourself.

WordPerfect includes several *paper definitions* along with the information it stores for your printer. Each definition includes the width and length of the paper, as well as its orientation and method of feeding through the printer.

To change page sizes:

1. Place the cursor in the first page of the document.

2. Select Layout ➤ Page (or press Shift+F8, P).

3. Select Paper Size/Type to display the Paper Size/Type dialog box, as shown in the figure.

4. Scroll the Paper Name list box and select from the available options.

5. Click on Select (or press Enter) to accept the selected size.

6. Click on OK.

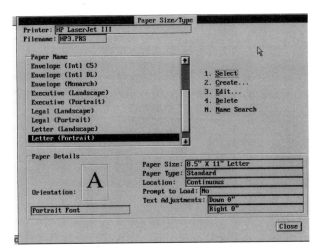

The Page Size/Type dialog box

Read what you need

TIP Beware of your position!

When you change page sizes, WordPerfect inserts a page size code at the beginning of the page in which the insertion point is located. If your document is more than one page long, make sure you are on the first page you want to format.

TIP Read the paper details

When you select a paper size in the Paper Name dialog box, a description of the page definition appears in the Paper Details box. Check the specifics of the definition carefully to make sure the definition and orientation are correct. If any details are not correct, you must edit the definition.

TIP Changing individual pages

To change the size of just one page in a document, place the cursor on that page, then select a new size. If you want following pages to print on the default size, place the cursor on the next page, then select Letter (Portrait) in the Paper Size/Type dialog box.

Printing an Envelope with a Letter

WordPerfect makes it easy for you to create envelopes for your letters. In a few keystrokes, you can format and print an envelope using an address you've already typed on screen.

To print an envelope:

1. Type the letter, including the inside address.

2. Select the complete mailing address in the letter.

3. Select Layout ➤ Envelope (or press Alt+F12) to display the Envelope dialog box, as shown in the figure.

4. Check the mailing address. If it is incorrect, select the Mailing Address box, edit the address, then press F7.

5. To include your return address, select the Return Address box, type your address, then press F7.

6. Check the envelope size. If it is incorrect, pull down the list box and select from defined envelope forms for your printer.

7. Click on Insert to place the envelope at the end of your document, separated from the text with a page break, or select Print to print the envelope immediately.

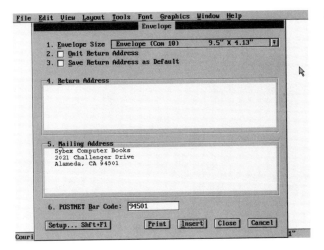

■ *The Envelope dialog box*

POSTNET Bar Codes

To insert a bar code, select POSTNET Bar Code in the Envelop dialog box, then enter a 5- or 9-digit zip code. To have WordPerfect insert the code automatically, select Setup (or press Shift+F1) from the Envelope dialog box, then choose Automatically Create Bar Code. Click on OK to return to the Envelope dialog box. When you next open the Envelope dialog box, the zip code in the selected address will appear in the POSTNET Bar Code box.

Setting envelope default values

The return address you enter in the Envelope dialog box is only used for the current document. To use the address for all envelopes, select Save Return Address as Default. Select Omit Return Address to skip it for the current envelope.

Do it fast

To display the Envelope dialog box, click on the Envelope button.

Read what you need

It's So Easy...   See Page...

Lesson 12

Enhancing Your Pages

This lesson will show you how to add some finishing touches to your document to make it even more effective. You'll learn how to use headers, footers, and page numbers to identify the document. That way, if individual pages get separated from the document, the reader will have little trouble locating their source. You'll also learn how to use watermarks to identify your documents as your own.

Creating Headers and Footers

A *header* prints specified lines of text at the top of every page. *Footers* do the same at the bottom. Headers and footers will not appear on the screen, except in page view and Print Preview.

To insert a header or footer:

1. Place the insertion point on the first page you want to contain the header or footer.

2. Select Layout ➤ Header/Footer/Watermark to display the dialog box in the figure. You can have two different headers and two different footers, known as *A* and *B*.

3. Select A or B.

4. Select All Pages, Even Pages, or Odd Pages.

5. Click on Create. The screen clears to display the Header/Footer Creation window.

6. Type the text of the header and footer.

7. Press F7.

To delete a header or footer, reveal codes and delete its code. To edit a header or footer, select Layout ➤ Header/Footer/Watermark, select either Headers or Footers, select A or B, and click on Edit.

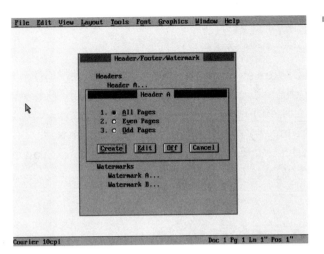

■ *The Header/Footer/*
  Watermark dialog box

 TIP ## Instant page numbering

In a header or footer, press Ctrl+P to insert the page number. Pages will
be numbered consecutively.

 TIP ## Alternating headers and footers

Coordinate A and B to print them on alternating pages. Select Odd Pages
for one, Even Pages for the other. But do not set both for the same page—
they may overlap on the same line.

 TIP ## When space is tight

Headers and footers print in the text area, not in the margins, reducing
the number of text lines on the page. To change the distance of text to the
header or footer, enter a measurement at the Space Below Header and
Space Below Footer options.

Inserting Watermarks

If you hold a fine sheet of paper up to the light, you may see a watermark faintly in the background. Watermarks usually contain the paper's manufacturer or brand name. You can use watermarks yourself to subtly promote your company name, logo, or a special message.

A WordPerfect watermark prints as a 25% shade. You can print watermarks on every page or on alternating pages.

To insert a watermark:

1. Place the insertion point at the start of the line where you want the watermark to appear.

2. Select Layout ➤ Header/Footer/Watermark.

3. Select Watermark A or Watermark B.

4. Select All Pages, Even Pages, or Odd Pages.

5. Click on Create.

6. Select Layout ➤ Justification ➤ Center.

7. Type the text of the watermark. It will appear in gray print. A sample watermark is shown in the figure.

8. Press F7.

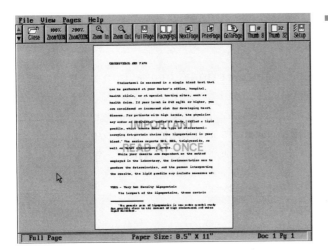

*Read
what
you
need*

 TIP **How watermarks work**

A watermark prints in gray, "under" the other text on the page. Unless you have a color printer, you can only print one color at a time. So the watermark is actually printed in the same color ink as the text but in a 25% tone—a series of dots only one quarter as dense as the dots that make up other characters.

 TIP **Sudden impact**

Format the text of the watermark using a large font size. Once you learn how to use WordPerfect's powerful graphics features, you can add drawings, pictures, and other graphic elements to your watermarks for dramatic effects.

 TIP **Can't see it?**

Watermarks do not appear on the screen except in Print Preview.

Page Numbers

A page number can be printed by itself on every page, even without including it in a header or footer. You can select the position of the number, include text such as *This is Page 30,* and even change the number that will be printed. Like headers and footers, the page number will not appear on the screen except in page view and Print Preview.

▪ To number pages:

1. Place the insertion point on the first page you want to contain the page number.

2. Select Layout ➤ Page ➤ Page Numbering.

3. Select Page Number Position to display the dialog box shown in the figure.

4. Select the position, from options 1 to 9.

5. Click on OK three times to return to the document.

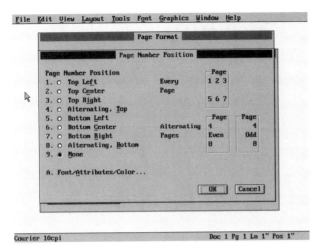

■ *The Page Number Position options*

Oops! Headers versus page numbers

A page number set for the top of the page will print on the same line as a header. A number set for the bottom will print on the same line as a footer. Be careful if you set both.

TIP Inserting a page number

The Insert Formatted Page Number option in the Page Numbering dialog box simply places the page number at the position of the insertion point in the text. This does not turn on page numbering, but prints the page number at that one location only.

TIP Changing page numbers

Suppose you have a 50-page document, followed by an appendix. If you turn on page numbers at the start of the document, the first page of the appendix will be numbered 51. To number the appendix separately, place the insertion point on its first page and select Layout ➤ Page ➤ Page Numbering ➤ Page Number. Select New Number and enter 1.

Customizing Page Numbers

You can enhance page numbering by adding text, such as *This is Page 2*, or by numbering pages in letters or roman numerals. Lowercase roman numerals, for example, are often used for frontmatter, such as a table of contents or introduction.

To customize page numbers:

1. Select Layout ➤ Page ➤ Page Numbering ➤ Page Number Format.

2. Enter text before the [page #] code, such as **Page [page #]**.

3. Select Page Number.

4. Pull down the Numbering Method list (shown in the figure) and select Numbers, Lower Letters, Upper Letters, Lower Roman, or Upper Roman.

5. Click on OK.

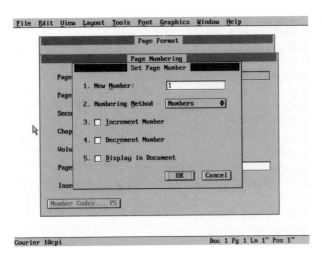

■ *The Set Page Number dialog box*

  The numbering position must be set

Selecting custom number options does not turn on page numbering. You must still select a number position.

  Order does not matter

You can turn on numbering and select options in any order.

  Location, location, location

WordPerfect inserts page number and format codes at the start of the page on which the insertion point is located. Before selecting custom options, place the insertion point on the first page containing the number you want to customize. For example, to number the appendix using roman numerals, place the insertion point on the first page of the appendix before selecting options.

Read what you need

Suppressing Page Elements

We usually do not place headers and footers on cover letters and title pages. Luckily, WordPerfect lets you *suppress* headers, footers, and page numbers on specific pages.

To suppress page elements:

1. Place the insertion point on the page where you wish to suppress headers, footers, or page numbers.

2. Select Layout ➤ Page ➤ Suppress to show the Suppress dialog box, as shown in the figure.

3. Select each of the items you want to suppress.

4. Click on OK.

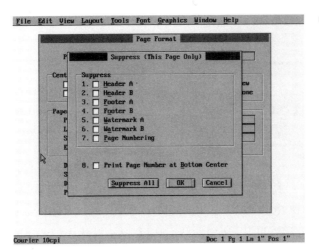

■ *The Suppress dialog box*

How Suppress works

Selecting an item for suppression suspends it from printing on the current page. Other pages are not affected.

All or nothing

Select Suppress All to suppress all of the listed elements—headers, footers, watermarks, and page numbers.

Retaining a page number

The Print Page Number at Bottom Center option prints a page number at the bottom center even if headers, footers, and other page numbering have been suppressed. Use this option if your header or footer contains a page number and you want to suppress the item but still number the page.

Let's Do It!

Formatting can add impact to even the simplest document. By adjusting the appearance of characters, lines, paragraphs, and pages, you make your document attractive and enjoyable to read.

Changing the Appearance of Characters

Let's start by formatting characters. We'll type some text, use underlining, change fonts and point size, and add a graphic symbol.

1. Start WordPerfect and type the following text:

```
The History of Tae Kwon Do


     While modern Tae Kwon Do can trace some of
its style to Chaun Fa, its history goes back over
2000 years. Ruins of the Koguryo dynasty from 37
BC were discovered in Korea with figures
positioned in poses resembling Tae Kwon Do
movements.
     Before the Korean nation was formed, the
peninsula was divided into three warring
kingdoms: Koguryo, Silla, and Paikche. Silla
finally prevailed, and in 668 AD the three
kingdoms united. It was during that period that
the martial art known as Tae Kyon developed.
     Silla was overthrown in 935 and became the
kingdom of Koryo, from which the name Korea is
derived. Over the years, however, interest in
martial arts declined, especially in the Yi
dynasty that was founded in 1392.
```

2. Select the words *Tae Kwon Do* in the first sentence of the first paragraph.

3. Select Font ➤ Underline.

4. Place the insertion point at the start of the document.

5. Select Font ➤ Font to display the Font dialog box.

6. Pull down the Font list.

7. Select one of the available fonts—preferably a scalable font marked Type 1, Speedo, or TrueType.

8. Pull down the Size list.

9. Select 14, if it is available.

10. Click on OK.

Now we'll change the relative size of the title.

11. Select the title, *The History of Tae Kwon Do*.

12. Select Font ➤ Size/Position ➤ Very Large. If the title word-wraps to a second line, select it again and choose the Large relative size.

13. Place the insertion point at the end of the document.

14. Press Enter twice.

Finally, we'll insert a graphic character.

15. Select Font ➤ WP Characters.

16. Type **5,80**.

17. Select Insert to insert a graphic star.

18. Select the star character.

19. Select Font ➤ Size/Position ➤ Extra Large. Your document should now look like Figure 3.1.

20. Select File ➤ Print/Fax ➤ Print to print the document.

21. Select File ➤ Save to save the document.

22. Type **TKD** and click on OK.

23. Select File ➤ Exit WP ➤ Exit if you're not ready to go on.

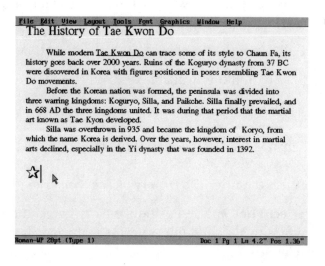

■ FIGURE 3.1:
The TKD document

Formatting Lines

Now let's change the line spacing, center the title, and justify the text. Here's how:

1. Open the document named **TKD** if it is not already on your screen.

2. Place the insertion point at the start of the document.

3. Select Layout ➤ Line ➤ Line Spacing.

4. Type **2**.

5. Click on OK.

6. Place the insertion point at the start of the title.

7. Select Layout ➤ Alignment ➤ Center (or press Shift+F6).

8. Place the insertion point in front of the first paragraph.

9. Select Layout ➤ Justification ➤ Full.

10. Select File ➤ Save.

11. Select File ➤ Exit WP ➤ Exit if you're not ready to go on.

Formatting Paragraphs

Indenting paragraphs helps call attention to specific portions of text. It also breaks up long sections of text, making them easier to read and more pleasing to the eye.

In this exercise, we'll practice formatting paragraphs by creating three different indentation styles, starting with a hanging indentation.

1. Open the document named **TKD** if it is not already on your screen.

2. Place the insertion point at the far left in front of the first paragraph, before the tab space.

3. Select Layout ➤ Alignment ➤ Hanging Indent. The text shifts to the $\frac{1}{2}$-inch position.

4. Type **1.** to number the paragraph.

5. Place the insertion point at the left margin in front of the second paragraph, before the tab space.

6. Select Layout ➤ Alignment ➤ Indent → (or press F4).

7. Press Del to remove the tab space.

8. Place the insertion point in front of the last paragraph, this time after the tab space.

9. Select Layout ➤ Alignment ➤ Indent → ← (or press Shift+F4). The paragraph is indented $1/2$-inch on both the left and right and the tab no longer affects the first line.

10. Select File ➤ Close ➤ No to clear the window without saving the document.

11. Select File ➤ Exit WP ➤ Exit if you're not ready to go on.

Formatting Pages

Page formats affect the entire page. You can set margins to change the amount of text that fits on the page and change page sizes to print on different sizes of paper or envelopes.

Let's widen the left and right margins, and print the document on legal-size paper.

1. Open the document named **TKD** if it is not already on your screen.

2. Select Layout ➤ Margins.

3. Select Left Margin, type **2**, then press Tab to select Right Margin.

4. Type **2**, then press Enter.

5. Click on OK.

6. Select Layout ➤ Page ➤ Paper Size/Type.

7. Scroll the list and select Legal (Portrait), if it is available.

8. Choose Select.

9. Click on OK.

10. Select File ➤ Print Preview to look at the document in Print Preview. Your document should look like Figure 3.2.

11. Select File ➤ Close (or press F7).

12. Select File ➤ Close ➤ No to clear the window without saving the document.

13. Select File ➤ Exit WP ➤ Exit if you're not ready to go on.

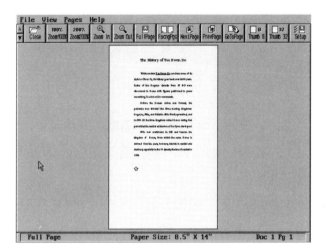

■ FIGURE 3.2:
The reformatted document with wide margins on legal-size paper

Adding Headers, Footers, and Page Numbers

You can add some finishing touches to your documents with headers, footers, and page numbers. But don't overdo it! Make them simple so they don't distract from the text.

Follow these steps to add a header and page number to the TKD document.

1. Open the document named **TKD** if it is not already on your screen.

2. Select Layout ➤ Header/Footer/Watermark.

3. Select Header A.

4. Select Create.

5. Type your name.

6. Select Layout ➤ Alignment ➤ Flush Right (or press Alt+F6).

7. Select Tools ➤ Date ➤ Text.

8. Press F7 to return to the document. Remember, you only see headers in page view and Print Preview.

9. Select Layout ➤ Page ➤ Page Numbering ➤ Page Number Position.

10. Select Bottom Center.

11. Click on OK three times to return to the document.

12. Select File ➤ Print Preview. Your document should look like Figure 3.3.

13. Select File ➤ Close to return to the document.

14. Select File ➤ Save.

15. Select File ➤ Close to clear the window.

16. Select File ➤ Exit WP ➤ Exit if you're not ready to go on.

Creating Tables

When you want to make a point with numbers, place them in a table. A table makes direct impact by letting the numbers stand out. A table draws the eye, getting immediate attention and placing the reader's focus just where you want it.

Let's create a small table.

1. Select Layout ➤ Tables ➤ Create (or press Alt+F7, T).

2. Type 3, then press Tab.

3. Type 4, then click on OK to display the Table Editor.

4. Click on Close.

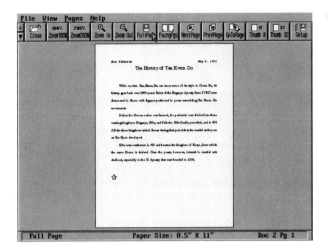

■ FIGURE 3.3:
*The TKD document
with a header and
page number in Print
Preview*

5. Press → to move to cell B1.

6. Select Layout ➤ Alignment ➤ Center (or press Shift+F6) and type **1993**.

7. Press → to move to cell C1.

8. Select Layout ➤ Alignment ➤ Center (or press Shift+F6) and type **1994**.

9. Move to cell A2, and type **Income**. (Turn ahead to Figure 3.4 if you need help finding the correct position for *Income*.)

10. Press → and type **64,500**.

11. Press → and type **75,600**.

12. Move to cell A2, and type **Expenses**.

13. Press → and type **14,250**.

14. Press → and type **13,780**.

15. Move to cell A3, and type **Profit**. (We'll add the profit amounts later.)

16. Select File ➤ Save.

17. Type **Profit** and click on OK.

18. Select File ➤ Close.

Using Formulas to Create a Spreadsheet

When we created the table named Profit, we didn't manually calculate and insert the net profit amounts. That's because we can have Word-Perfect do this for us automatically by using formulas. Let's add the formulas now and format the calculated cells.

1. Open the document named **Profit**.

2. Place the insertion point in cell B4 (the one below the cell containing 14,250).

3. Select Layout ➤ Tables ➤ Edit.

4. Select Formula.

5. Type **B2-B3** and click on OK.

Notice that the result, 50250, does not have a comma separating the thousands. Let's take care of that.

6. Select the Cell command at the bottom of the screen to display cell format options.

7. Select Number Type to display additional options.

8. Select Use Commas, then click on OK twice. The result now appears as 50,250.

9. Select cell C4.

10. Select Formula.

11. Type **C2-C3** and click on OK.

12. Select the Cell ➤ Number Type ➤ Use Commas, then click on OK twice.

13. Select Close to display the table. It should look like Figure 3.4. If you change any of the income or expense amounts, click on Layout ➤ Tables ➤ Calculate All to recalculate the formulas.

14. Select File ➤ Save.

15. Select File ➤ Print/Fax ➤ Print.

16. Select File ➤ Close.

File	Edit	View	Layout	Tools	Font	Graphics	Window	Help

	1993	1994
Income	64,500	75,600
Expenses	14,250	13,780
Profit	50,250	61,820

=C2-C3   Cell C4 Doc 1 Pg 1 Ln 1.93" Pos 5.42"

■ FIGURE 3.4:
The formatted table

Working with Columns

Finally, let's see how easy it is to create newsletters. We'll use the TKD document, even though it really doesn't have enough text to fill up the page.

1. Open the document named **TKD**.

2. Place the insertion point in front of the first paragraph, below the title.

3. Select Layout ➤ Columns.

4. Select Number of Columns.

5. Type 3 and click on OK. The text under the title automatically adjusts to the default 1.83-inch column width.

6. Select File ➤ Print Preview. Figure 3.5 shows how your document should look.

7. Select File ➤ Close to exit Print Preview.

8. Select File ➤ Close ➤ No.

9. Select File ➤ Exit WP ➤ Exit.

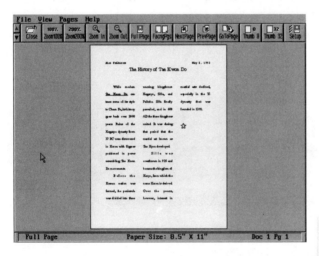

■ FIGURE 3.5:
The finished three-column newsletter

PART

4

Special WordPerfect Features

Congratulations! You've graduated from the SYBEX WordPerfect Academy. Now you're ready for graduate school.

In these lessons, you'll take the plunge into WordPerfect's most powerful features. Desktop publishing, form letters, and automating with macros are just a few of the things awaiting when you turn the page. Go ahead!

It's So Easy...   See Page...

Lesson 13

Working with Tables and Columns

WordPerfect has several handy features for creating documents in columnar and tabular formats. To create charts, spreadsheets, and other neatly ordered rows and columns of words or numbers, use WordPerfect's automatic table feature. Use the column feature to produce newsletters, resumes, and other documents of multiple columns across the page.

Creating a Table

Before creating a table, plan the number of rows and columns that you'll need. You'll be able to insert and delete rows and columns later—just like in a spreadsheet program—but WordPerfect will request a starting number when you begin.

To create a table:

1. Select Layout ➤ Tables ➤ Create (or press Alt+F7, T).

2. Type the number of columns you want, then press Enter.

3. Type the number of rows you want, then click on OK. WordPerfect will create a ruled table and place you in the Table Editor, as shown in the figure. You use the Table Editor to change the table structure, but not the text that goes into the table.

4. Click on Close to return to the document. The blank table appears in the document window.

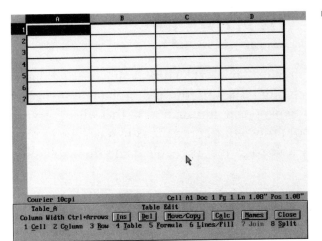

■ *The Table Editor*

 TIP

Table structure

Each *cell* in the table is referenced by its row and column numbers. The top left cell is A1. A two-row by five-column table would be referenced as follows:

	A	B	C	D	E
1	A1	B1	C1	D1	E1
2	A2	B2	C2	D2	E2

 TIP

Watch the status line

The right side of the status line will indicate the location of the insertion point. The left side will indicate the formula or function contained in the cell. (Formulas and functions are covered later in this lesson.)

Entering Data in Tables

Once you create a table's structure, you can enter data into it. Many tables have *labels* along the top row and in the leftmost column. The labels identify or explain the information in the other rows and columns. Don't worry about how your entry aligns in a cell, or in rows and columns. You'll be able to format the table using the Table Editor.

To enter data in cells:

1. Move to the cell you want to enter data into using any of these methods:

- Click on the cell with the mouse.
- Press ↑ and ↓ to move up and down columns.
- Press ←, →, Tab, and Shift+Tab to move across rows.

2. Type the data for the cell. The cell height will adjust automatically to the amount of text. *Do not press Enter to move to the next cell.* If you press Enter, the cell height will increase by one line. Press the Backspace key to delete the blank line.

File	Edit	View	Layout	Tools	Font	Graphics	Window	Help

YEAR	Gross Sales	Cost	Net Profit
1995	560,000	7,000	80
1996	1,250,000	10,000	125
1997	490,000	7,000	70
1998	1,800,000	12,000	150
1999	960,000	4,800	200
2000	1,215,000	9,000	135

Courier 10cpi   Doc 1 Pg 1 Ln 1" Pos 1"

■ *A table complete with cell entries*

Read what you need

Word wrap in narrow cells

WordPerfect does not automatically adjust the cell width to accommodate text. If you type a word or number that's longer than the width of the cell, it will be inappropriately divided between two lines. Widen the cell as explained in "Using the Table Editor" later in this lesson.

Editing cells

To edit the data in a cell, move to the cell and use WordPerfect's normal editing techniques. Just be careful when you use the Del or Backspace keys to delete text. If you continue pressing the key after all of the text in the cell is deleted, the insertion point will move to the adjacent cell and delete text there.

Formatting cells

You can use options in the Layout and Font menus, or their equivalent shortcut keys, to format text in cells. To format entire an entire row or column, see "Using the Table Editor" later in this lesson.

Editing Tables

Once you create a table, you can add and delete rows, divide it into multiple tables, and even combine two tables into one. You can use the options in the Tables menu to make these and other changes.

To change the table:

1. Place the insertion point in any cell of the table.

2. Select Layout ➤ Tables to display the Tables pull-down menu, as shown in the figure.

3. Select the option you want from those listed below:

— *Insert Row:* Adds a row above the current row

— *Delete Row:* Deletes the current row

— *Join:* Combines the table with one immediately following it. The tables must have the same number of columns.

— *Split:* Splits the table into two at the current row, which becomes the first row of the new table.

— *Calculate All:* Recalculates formulas and functions that perform math on cell contents

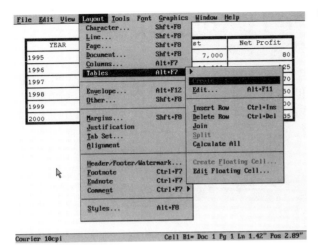

Trouble splitting and joining tables?

In order to combine two tables using the Join command, there must be no blank lines or text between them. If you split a table, the resulting tables appear with no blank spaces between them. To insert a blank line between tables, place the insertion point at the start of cell A1 in the second table, select Edit ➤ Reveal Codes (or press F11), then press ← to move the insertion point outside of the table. Press Enter to insert a blank line, then select Edit ➤ Reveal Codes (or press F11) to remove the code display.

 ## Making WordPerfect work faster

If you are working with a large table, WordPerfect may respond slowly as you scroll from section to section. Either work with the table in text view, or create the table in two or more sections, each section in a different document window. To combine the sections into a single table, copy the sections to one window, place them under each other—with no blank lines between them—and use the Join command.

Using the Table Editor

While you can change the structure of a table using options in the Layout ➤ Tables menu, the Table Editor gives you complete control over the table's format. Using the Table Editor, you can quickly format selected cells or entire rows and columns.

To use the Table Editor:

1. Place the insertion point in any cell of the table.

2. Select Layout ➤ Tables ➤ Edit (or press Alt+F11).

3. Place the insertion point in the cell, row, or column you want to edit.

4. Press Ctrl+→ to make a column wider, or press Ctrl+← to make a column narrower.

5. Use the options at the bottom of the screen to change the format or structure of the table.

Select Cell, Column, Row, or Table to change the style and position of these elements. Select Formula to insert formulas and functions. Select Lines/Fills to change the type of lines and background. Select Join to combine selected cells or Split to divide a selected cell into two. Select Ins or Del to insert or delete rows or columns. Use Move to move or copy cells, rows, or columns. Select Calc to recalculate table formulas and functions. Use Names to give cells or ranges of cells names for use in formulas and functions.

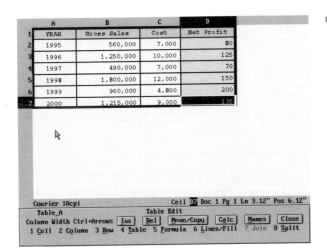

■ *The Table Editor showing formatted cells and adjusted column widths*

Select the cell first

WordPerfect may respond slowly when you scroll through a large table in the Table Editor. To speed things up, select the cell you want to format before displaying the Table Editor.

Changing the order of rows and columns

To change the position of rows or columns, display the Table Editor, then select any cell in the row or column you want to change. Click on Move/ Copy (or press Ctrl+F4) to display a dialog box. Select either Row or Column, then select either Move or Copy. If you select Move, the row or column will be deleted. Next, select a cell where you want to insert the row or column and press Enter. WordPerfect inserts columns to the left of the current columns. Rows are inserted above the current row.

For quick access

You can display the Table Editor by clicking on the TblEdit button in the button bar.

Read what you need

Performing Math with Formulas

If you want to include totals, averages, or other mathematical results in a table, you can use *formulas* to compute the numbers for you. Formulas can make your table a full-fledged *spreadsheet*, an electronic version of an accountant's ledger.

Though a full explanation of spreadsheets is beyond the scope of this book, the following procedure and the example in the "Let's Do It!" section will give you a taste of what spreadsheets can do. Suppose you have a table showing your income and expenses for the year, such as the table in the figure. You can use formulas to total the income and expense categories, and other formulas to subtract the totals to obtain your net profit. If you enter your formulas correctly, WordPerfect will calculate the totals and net amounts for you.

To enter a formula into a cell:

1. Place the insertion point in the cell in which you want to insert the formula.

2. Select Layout ➤ Tables ➤ Edit to display the Table Editor.

3. Select Formula.

4. Type the formula. (If you don't know how to create a spreadsheet formula, see "Cell References" on the facing page for more information.)

5. Click on OK. The results of the calculation appear in the cell.

If you later change the value in a cell referenced in the formula, you must tell WordPerfect to recalculate the results.

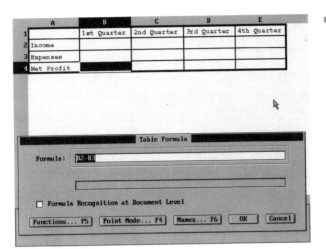

Operators and cell references

A formula can include mathematical operators, numeric values, and *cell references*. If you are writing a simple equation, just type in the equation as you would on a calculator, using + for addition, - for subtraction, * for multiplication, and / for division. To create a more flexible formula, you can reference a cell by its location in the table. For example, entering **B2-B3** in cell B4 will calculate and display the difference between cell B2 and B3 in cell B4, no matter what numbers are in B1 and B2. For more information on formulas, see your WordPerfect manual.

Formula and function errors

If two question marks appear in the cell, your formula (or function) contains an error. Select the cell and display the Formula dialog box. A brief description of the error will appear under the Formula box.

Performing Math with Functions

While formulas can be quite powerful, those that reference a large number of cells or that use a complex equation can require quite a bit of typing. To save much of that work, you can choose from a list of mathematical, statistical, logical, date and financial *functions*.

A function is a formula already built into WordPerfect. You only have to name the function and tell WordPerfect what cells, or group of cells, to use for the calculation. For example, the average function is AVE(list), where *list* is a range or series of cells. So AVE(B1:B10) will calculate and display the average of those ten cells from column B. Notice that the first and last cells in the group are separated with a colon. That's a lot easier than typing (**B1+B2+B3+B4+B5+B6+B7+B8+B9+B10)/10**!

To enter a function into a cell:

1. Place the insertion point in the cell in which you want to insert the function.

2. Select Layout ➤ Tables ➤ Edit to display the Table Editor.

3. Select Formula. Then select Functions (or press F5) to display the dialog box shown in the figure. The dialog box will display a brief description of the highlighted function.

4. Scroll the list and double-click on the function, or select the function and click on Insert. The Formula dialog box reappears with a sample of the function's syntax listed beneath the Formula box.

5. Edit the function in the Formula box to insert the cells or range of cells.

6. Click on OK.

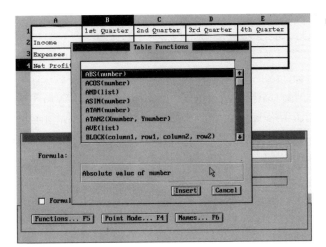

■ *The Function list box*

If you're new to functions

Functions can be a confusing subject when you're new to them. Word-Perfect provides about 100 functions from which you can select, far too many to cover in a book of this length. Many require some mathematical, statistical, or financial knowledge to use correctly. For example, financial functions include those which calculate depreciation, future value, net present value, internal rate of return, and periodic payment. If you would like to know more about functions, refer to your WordPerfect manual.

Entering Functions Manually

If you know the function you want to use, type it directly into the Formula box. This saves the trouble of display and scrolling the function list.

Creating Newspaper Columns

If you're responsible for producing a newsletter or some other multi-column document, you'll want to take advantage of WordPerfect's built-in Newspaper Column feature. *Newspaper columns* automatically run from one column to the next on the page, from left to right. When the far right column is filled, text moves to the left column on the next page.

To type newspaper columns:

1. Select Layout ➤ Columns (or press Alt+F7, C) to see the Text Columns dialog box, as shown in the figure.

2. Select Number of Columns.

3. Type the number of columns desired.

4. You can change the spacing between columns by entering the measurement at the Distance Between Columns option.

5. Click on OK.

6. Type your text. You can move between columns by pressing Ctrl+Home, → to move to the column on the right or Ctrl+Home, ← to move to the column on the left.

Before creating multiple columns, you may want to type your document using the default single column format and save it to your disk. Then place the cursor where you want the columns to begin and experiment with columns. You can always start over by revealing codes, deleting the Column Definition code, and trying another format.

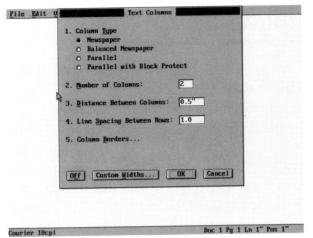

■ *The Text Columns dialog box*

Mixing single and multiple columns

Before typing columns, type any desired single-column text, such as a title or introductory paragraph, then turn on Columns and type the rest of the text. To type single-column text again, press Ctrl+Enter to end the last column and select Layout ➤ Columns ➤ Off.

Avoid justification

Fully justified columns, especially narrow ones, may have unsightly spaces. Hyphenate if you must justify.

Instant columns

You can create columns from the ribbon by pulling down the Column list and selecting from 1 to 4 columns, starting at the position of the insertion point.

Creating Parallel Columns

In some cases you don't want text to flow freely from column to column, because text on the left refers directly to text on the right. This format is used often in job resumes, where the left column contains employment dates, and the right column includes the employer and job responsibilities.

These are called *parallel columns*. With parallel columns, you enter the text in blocks: the first text on the left, then its corresponding text on the right; the second text on the left, then its corresponding text on the right, etc. Press Ctrl+Enter to end a block and move to the other column.

To create parallel columns:

1. Select Layout ➤ Columns ➤ Parallel.

2. Select Number of Columns, enter the column number, then press Enter.

3. For unequal columns, select Custom Widths, then enter the width of each column.

4. Click on OK.

5. Type a left-hand column.

6. Press Ctrl+Enter.

7. Type a right-hand column.

8. Press Ctrl+Enter.

```
File  Edit  View  Layout  Tools  Font  Graphics  Window  Help
      Team            Function           Members

       A              Survey             Wilma Wilson, Leader
                                         John Smith, Marla Halley, Kim
                                         Lee, Garry DelAbote

       B              Documentation      Paul Harvey, Leader
                                         Nancy Chesin, Don Siravo, Neal
                                         Welsh

       C              Data Entry         Delora Sallie, Leader
                                         J. B. Taylor, Corey Feldman,
                                         Howard Sturm|




                                    ▷

Univers 14pt                     Col 3 Doc 1 Pg 1 Ln 3.66" Pos 5.81"
```

■ *Parallel columns*

Read what you need

 Moving between columns

As with newspaper columns, you can move from column to column by pressing Ctrl+Home, → and Ctrl+Home, ←.

 Block protection

Parallel columns can be regular or block-protected. Block-protected parallel columns are kept next to each other. If the text in one column extends into the new page, both columns will be carried over so they start on that page. Regular parallel columns, on the other hand, will span a page break.

 Distance between rows

WordPerfect inserts a blank line when you press Ctrl+Enter to end the rightmost parallel column. To change the spacing, enter a number in the Line Spacing Between Rows prompt in the Text Columns dialog box. For example, enter **0** for no spacing or **2** for two blank lines.

It's So Easy...

Lesson 14

Enhancing Documents with Lines and Boxes

Sometimes it takes more than words to capture a reader's attention. With WordPerfect's graphics features, you can enhance your documents' appearance by adding lines, borders, and boxes. You can even draw freehand lines and shapes. With a bit of practice, you can create truly dazzling documents.

Adding Vertical and Horizontal Lines

Horizontal and vertical lines are great for separating different sections of text or adding some visual perspective. You can use the options on the Graphics Lines menu to insert lines before or after text or along the margins. If you really want a page to stand out, you can add a horizontal line to a header or footer.

■ To create a line:

1. Place the insertion point where you want to insert the line.

2. Select Graphics ➤ Graphics Lines ➤ Create to display the Create Graphics Line dialog box, as shown in the figure.

3. Pull down the Line Orientation box.

4. Select Horizontal or Vertical.

5. Click on OK.

The default horizontal line is $6\frac{1}{2}$ inches long, centered between the left and right margins. The default vertical line is 9 inches long down the left side of the page. Graphics lines will not appear in text view.

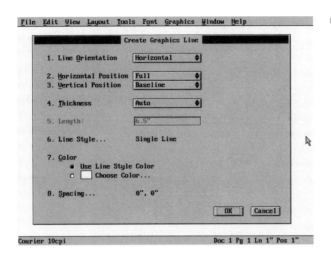

■ *The Create Graphics Line dialog box*

 TIP   **More Graphics Line options**

You can customize the appearance of your lines by changing the options in the Create Graphics Line dialog box, as follows:

— *Horizontal Position* sets the position of the line in relation to the left and right margins.

— *Vertical Position* sets the position of the line in relation to the text line at the insertion point.

— *Thickness* sets the thickness of the line in inches or points.

— *Length* sets the length of the line in inches or points.

— *Line Style* changes the type of line or creates multiple lines.

— *Color* changes the color of the line.

— *Spacing* sets the distance of text above and below horizontal lines, and the distance from the left margin for vertical lines.

Changing the Size and Position of Lines

Once a line has been inserted, you can use the mouse to change its size, shape, and position. (Using the keyboard, you can only move and size lines from within the Graphics Lines dialog box.)

To change the size or position of a line:

1. Place the mouse pointer on the line.

2. Click the left mouse button. The line will be surrounded by eight small black squares, called *handles*, and a dotted *selection box*, as in the figure.

3. To move the line, point inside the selection box and drag the mouse.

4. To change the size of the box:

   — Drag the center handle on top or bottom to change the height of the graphic.

   — Drag the center handle on the left or right to change the width of the graphic.

   — Drag a handle on a corner to change both the width and height at the same time.

As you drag the mouse, the selection box moves with it. Release the mouse button when the line is the desired size or at the desired location.

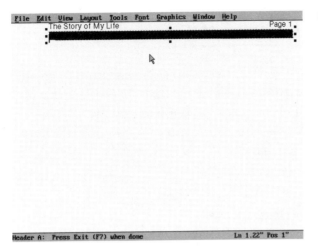

■ *A selected line in a header*

Read what you need

 Where are the handles?

When you select a thin line, you may not be able to see all eight handles.

 Deleting lines

To delete a line, select it and press Del, Y.

 Editing lines

To edit a line, double-click on the line to display the Edit Graphics Line dialog box (or select Graphics ➤ Graphics Lines ➤ Edit, enter the line number, and select Edit Line.) Change the orientation, position, and other settings, then click on OK.

Drawing Freehand Lines

You can use WordPerfect's Line Draw feature to create freehand drawings of horizontal and vertical lines. WordPerfect will draw lines following the path of the insertion point as you press →, ←, ↑, and ↓. You cannot draw diagonal lines, but you can draw straight lines, squares, rectangles, and other shapes.

To draw lines:

1. Place the insertion point where you want to begin drawing.

2. Select Graphics ➤ Line Draw (or press Ctrl+F3, 5) to display the Line Draw dialog box, as in the figure.

3. Press the arrow keys to draw a line following the path of the insertion point. You cannot use the mouse to draw lines.

4. Click on Close.

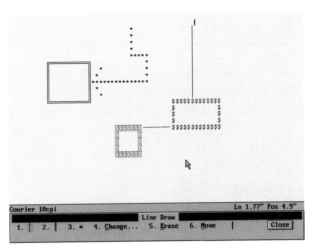

■ *The Line Draw dialog box. The lines in the document were created using the default single-line style as well as alternate drawing characters.*

▼ TIP   To delete freehand lines

A line created with Line Draw is actually a series of individual graphic characters. Delete each character individually, or select any portion of the line and press Del.

▼ TIP   More Line Draw options

The following options are available from the Line Draw dialog box:

Select	To
2	Draw double lines
3	Draw in a series of asterisks
4 Change	To select a character other than the asterisk
5 Erase	Erase an existing line as you move the insertion point over it
6 Move	Move the insertion point without drawing a line

Creating a Page Border

You can create eye-catching announcements, certificates, and advertisements by creating page borders. You can place a border around a single page, or around every page in your document—all with a few clicks of the mouse!

To create a page border:

1. Select Graphics ➤ Borders ➤ Page to display the Create Page Border dialog box.

2. Select Border Style to select from preset line types.

3. Select Fill Style to select a gray shade to print in the background of the page.

4. Select Customize to set the line thickness, corner type, color, and shadow of the border.

5. Click on OK.

To see the entire border, change to page view or Print Preview.

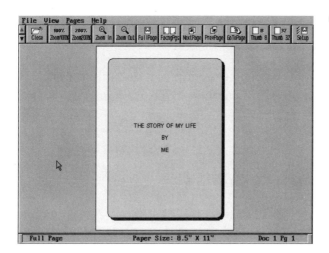

■ *A customized page border in Print Preview*

Borders on multipage documents

By default, page borders appear on every page of a multipage document, starting with the page on which the insertion point is located. To turn off the border on subsequent pages, select Graphics ➤ Borders ➤ Page ➤ Off.

Other border options

Select Graphics ➤ Borders ➤ Column to add lines between or around columns in newsletters. Select Graphics ➤ Borders ➤ Styles to customize the way borders appear. See Lesson 17 for more details on editing graphics.

Creating Boxed Text

If you want a particular section of a document to stand out, you can place it in a box. You can box an entire paragraph or just a title or headline.

To create boxed text:

1. Select the text you wish to place in a box.

2. Select Graphics ➤ Borders ➤ Paragraph to display the Create Paragraph Border dialog box.

3. Select Border Styles to select from preset line types.

4. Select Fill Style to select a gray shade to print in the background of the page.

5. Select Customize to set the line styles, corner type, color, and shadow of the border.

6. Click on OK.

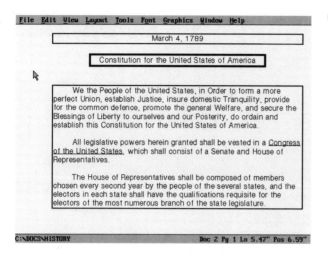

■ *Paragraph borders showing the effect of page margins*

 ### There's one large box!

If you do not select text first, the box will surround all of the text on the page. To resize the box, place the insertion point where you want the box to stop and select Graphics ➤ Borders ➤ Paragraph ➤ Off.

 ### Box width

By default, boxes extend from the right to left margin, even if you place a one-word title centered on the page in the box. To make a narrower box, change the page margins for the text. Just remember to reset the margins following the box.

Read what you need

It's so easy...

Lesson 15

Creating Form Letters

If you work in a business office, you're probably well aware of the importance of form letters. A well-designed form letter allows you to send the same information to many different people, but with a personal touch—so the greeting line reads *Dear Ms. White* or *Dear Mr. Apple*, rather than the cold and boring *Dear Sir or Madame*.

But you don't need to run a business to take advantage of form letters. Aren't there repetitive letters or other documents that you need? How about responses to classified ads, requests for information, or letters of complaint? Perhaps you are sending notes, thank-you letters, or invitations to family members or friends. Except for some personalized text, such as the name and address, each letter has the same words. So save time and use a form letter!

Creating a Data File for Form Documents

The first task in writing a form letter is to create the data file. A *data file* contains all the pertinent information about a group of items, such as the name, address, and other information about clients or employees you are sending form letters to.

Picture the data file as an electronic version of an index card file. Every card, called a *record*, contains all the data about one recipient of your form letter. Each record has several pieces of information, such as the name of the recipient, his or her street, city, and state. Each piece of information is called a *field*.

To create a data file:

1. Select Tools ➤ Merge ➤ Define ➤ Data [Table].

2. Select Create A Table With Field Names.

3. For each field, type a field name, such as Client Name, and press Enter.

4. Click on OK. A table will appear with the field names in the first row.

5. Type the contents of each field, then press Tab. WordPerfect will word-wrap the entry if it is wider than the cell. Don't worry—this will not affect how the information appears in the form letter. The figure shows an example of a filled-in table.

6. Save the table.

File Edit View Layout Tools Font Graphics Window Help

Client	Address	City	State	Zip	Greeting
Jean Kelly	17 West Fifth St.	Wilson	PA	19110	Jean
Kay Riser	1982 Alameda Blvd.	Alameda	CA	94501	Kay
John Acme	76 First Ave.	Philadelphia	PA	19116	John

C:\DOCS\CLIENTS   Cell F4 Doc 2 Pg 1 Ln 2.43" Pos 7.05"

■ *The completed data file*

Read what you need

 Adding rows

When you press Tab after typing the last field in the bottom row, Word-Perfect adds another row to the table. Do not press Enter.

 Data files as text

If each record has a large number of fields, it may become time-consuming to scroll table columns into view on the screen. Instead of using a data file table, create the file as a text document by selecting Tools ➤ Merge ➤ Define ➤ Data [Text] ➤ OK. Type each field on a separate line, ending each by pressing F9 to insert an ENDFIELD code. This tells WordPerfect when one field ends and the next one begins. At the end of each record, press Shift+F9, 2 to insert an ENDRECORD code and a hard page break. The code and page break designate the end of each record. You'll be able to see a large record at one time, without the need to scroll the screen horizontally.

Writing the Form Letter

Now that you have a database, you can create the document that contains the form letter. When you come to a place where you want a client's name and address or some other variable information to appear, you enter a field code giving the name of the field that you want inserted at that location. WordPerfect will insert the information from each record into the form letter during the merge process, which is discussed later in this lesson.

To write a form letter:

1. Select Tools ➤ Merge ➤ Define ➤ Form and click on OK twice.

2. Type the letter.

3. When you reach a location where you want to enter a field, press Shift+F9, 1; type the field name; and press Enter. The figure shows a form letter using the field names from the data file created in the previous exercise.

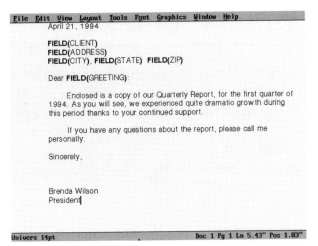

■ *A completed form document*

 TIP   ## Displaying field names

If you forget the field names, you can display them in a list box. Press Shift+F9, 1, then select List Field Names. Enter the name of the data file, then click on OK. Select the field you want to enter into the form letter.

 TIP   ## Merge codes

Unlike other codes used by WordPerfect, the field and merge codes used in form letters are displayed on the screen along with other text. As long as you print the documents using the Merge feature, the variable information, not the codes, will be printed. If you print the document using File ➤ Print, the codes will print as displayed and the variable information will not be inserted.

 TIP   ## Duplicate fields

You can include a field more than once in the same form letter.

Merging and Printing Form Documents

When you perform a merge, the variable information from each record in your data file is inserted in the appropriate place in the form letter you wrote. After one version of the letter is created, a page break is inserted and another letter containing another record is created, until all of the records have been used.

Newly merged documents can be printed immediately, saved on disk, or edited.

To merge form letters:

1. Select File ➤ New to clear the document window.

2. Select Tools ➤ Merge ➤ Run to display the Run Merge dialog box.

3. Type the name of the form letter file, then press Enter.

4. Type name of the data file, then press Enter.

5. Click on Merge.

The word *Merging* will appear on the status line as the letters are generated. The letters will be displayed on the screen only after all of the merging is completed. You can now print the letters or save them on disk.

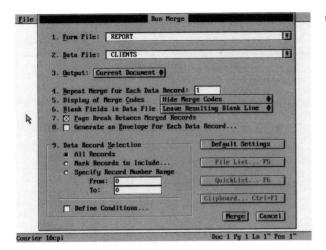

■ *The Run Merge dialog box showing Data File options*

🔑 TIP **Merging form documents to the printer**

To print form documents as they are merged, pull down the Output list in the Run Merge dialog box and select Printer. Each letter is printed as it is generated—they do not appear on screen and cannot be saved.

🔑 TIP Merge options

You can customize the merge by selecting Data File Options in the Run Merge dialog box. The box expands to display additional choices, as shown in the figure. Once selected, the expanded dialog box will appear automatically when you select Tools ➤ Merge ➤ Run until you close the document.

🔑 TIP Skipping blank address lines

Some addresses contain office numbers, post office boxes, or other information in addition to the street address. Leave the cell blank in the data file table for addresses that do not have this extra information. To avoid printing a blank line for empty fields, in the Run Merge dialog box, select Data File Options, pull down the Blank Fields in Data File list, and select Remove Resulting Blank Lines.

Printing Envelopes for Form Letters

If you are printing form letters, you can generate the envelopes at the same time by using the merge codes that make up the inside address. The envelopes will be inserted in a group following all of the form letters. Just keep the letters in order after they are printed so you can easily match them to the appropriate envelope!

▪ *To print form envelopes:*

1. Open the form letter file document.

2. Select the merge codes that represent the address, then select Edit ➤ Copy and Paste (or press Ctrl+Ins).

3. Select File ➤ Close to close the letter file, and then select Tools ➤ Merge ➤ Run to open the Run Merge dialog box.

4. Enter the form file and data file names.

5. Select Data File Options, if the options are not already displayed.

6. Select Generate an Envelope for Each Data Record to display the Envelope window.

7. Select the Mailing Address box, press Enter to insert the address codes, then press F7.

8. Select POSTNET Bar Code.

9. Type the name of the field containing the zip code—you do not need to use the field code.

10. Click on Insert, then click on Merge.

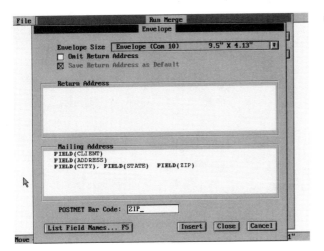

■ Merge codes for
printing envelopes

TIP   Where are the envelopes?

After the merge, the insertion point appears after the last letter. Scroll
down to display the envelopes.

Changing envelope settings

If you decide to change any of the envelope specifications after exiting
the Envelope dialog box, you can return to this dialog box by clicking on
Generate an Envelope for Each Data Record in the Run Merge dialog box.
You will have to reenter your addresses, bar code, and other settings.

I forgot the fields!

If you forget to select the codes for the inside address before opening the
Envelope dialog box, don't worry—there's no need to start over. While in
the Envelope dialog, select Mailing Address, press Shift+F9, select Field,
and select List Field Names. Double-click a field and click on OK to insert
the field in the inside address. Repeat this procedure until you've completed the address.

It's So Easy...   See Page...

Lesson 16

Tools to Improve Your Work

WordPerfect provides a number of special tools that go far beyond basic word processing functions. No matter what the task, these tools can make your work easier and faster. You can create macros to speed typing and menu selections, customize the button bar to suit your tastes, check your spelling, or use the thesaurus and grammar checker to improve your vocabulary and grammar.

Recording and Playing Macros

A *macro* is a special command that you create to automate repetitive tasks. If there is a particular task you do over and over in WordPerfect, such as formatting your page for each business letter you write, you can create a macro that records the keystrokes needed to format the page, and replay the recording in the future by simply pressing a few shortcut keys or typing the name of the macro. Macros can be used to repeat text, formatting commands, or any menu or dialog box selections.

To record a macro:

1. Select Tools ➤ Macro ➤ Record (or press Ctrl+F10) to display the Record Macro dialog box, as shown in the figure.

2. Type a name for the macro, or press Alt and a letter to assign it a shortcut key.

3. Click on OK.

4. Type the keystrokes or select the menu and dialog box options that you want to record in the macro. Note that while recording a macro, you cannot use the mouse to select text or to move the insertion point.

5. Select Tools ➤ Macro ➤ Stop.

To play a macro:

— Press the Alt+letter combination you assigned to the macro; or select Tools ➤ Macro ➤ Play (or press Alt+F10), type the macro name, then click on OK.

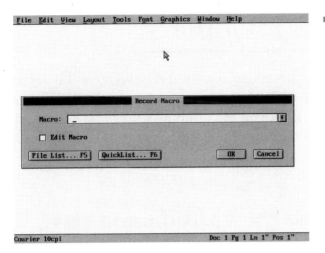

File Edit View Layout Tools Font Graphics Window Help

Record Macro

Macro: [_]

☐ Edit Macro

[File List... F5] [QuickList... F6]   [OK] [Cancel]

Courier 10cpi   Doc 1 Pg 1 Ln 1" Pos 1"

■ *The Record Macro*
dialog box

Read
what
you
need

FOR MORE... ### Creating Useful Macros

Macros can save you a lot of time, but they're tricky if you're new to
them. For some practice in creating a simple macro, turn to "Using
Macros" in the "Let's Do It!" section at the end of this part. Once you're
comfortable with macros, you may want to build a library of macros for
editing and formatting tasks you perform frequently. For example, if you
work in a legal office, you might want to create a macro that selects legal-
size paper or macros that insert standard "boilerplate" text for wills,
contracts, and other documents.

TIP ### To convert a WordPerfect 5.1 macro

If you want to use your WordPerfect 5.1 macros with version 6.0, you'll
have to convert them. From the DOS prompt in the WP60 directory,
type **MCV** and press Enter to run WordPerfect's macro convert program.
When a prompt appears, type the complete path and name of the version 5.1 macro minus the extension, as in **C:\WP51\MACRO1**, and press
Enter. Type the name you want to give to the 6.0 version of the macro
(again without the extension) and press Enter.

Using Button Bar Options

The button bar offers a quick and convenient way to execute the most popular WordPerfect commands, but its display may not be right for your needs. If so, you can customize the button bar by changing its position on the screen and the way commands are displayed on the button faces.

To change the position and style of the button bar:

1. Select View ➤ Button Bar Setup ➤ Options to display the Button Bar Options dialog box, as shown in the figure.

2. Select a position—the top, bottom, left, or right of the screen.

3. Select a style—both the picture and name of the function, the picture only, or name only.

4. Click on OK. The settings will now affect the appearance of whatever button bar you choose to display.

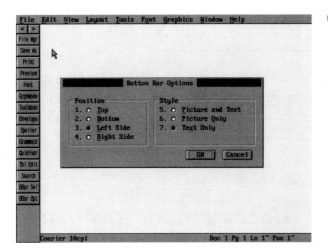

■ *The Button Bar Options dialog box with a customized button bar in the background*

  Get more buttons in text view

If you use the button bar in text view, consider changing its position to the left or right side of the screen. When on the top or bottom of the screen, you can only see six buttons and the arrows that scroll more buttons into view. When on the left or right, you can display up to 23 buttons.

  Text view options

In text view, you can only select to see the name; there are no options for displaying pictures or icons.

  The Print Preview button bar

The Print Preview button bar will not be affected by button bar options you select from the editing window. To change the Print Preview button bar, select File ➤ Print Preview, then select View ➤ Button Bar Setup ➤ Options.

Correcting Spelling Errors

To many WordPerfect users, the spelling checker is the most important tool the program provides. Typographical and spelling errors can occur no matter how careful you are. Save yourself some embarrassing moments by checking spelling before printing and distributing your document.

◼ To check a document for spelling:

1. Position the insertion point in the text you want to spell-check. If you do not want to check the entire document, place the insertion point on the word or page you want to check. To check a block of text, select the text first.

2. Select Tools ➤ Writing Tools ➤ Speller. A dialog box appears with options to select the amount of text you want to check. Options are Word, Page, Document, and From Cursor.

3. Select how much of the document you want to spell check. If you select Page, for example, WordPerfect will just check the page on which the insertion point is located. WordPerfect finds the first possible error and displays the Word not Found dialog box. Possible alternatives will be shown in the list box on the left.

4. Double-click on the correctly spelled word in the list (scroll the list if necessary) to replace the misspelled word, or select Skip in this Document to accept the word as it is spelled for the remainder of the session.

```
    The mutual  inductence  of two r-f coils with fields
interacting, is given by

          M = (L_A - L_o)/4
```

■ *The Word Not Found dialog box*

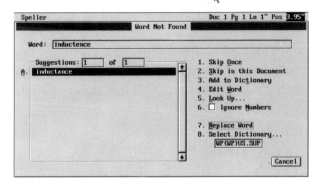

Read
what
you
need

Using the keyboard

To replace a misspelled word from the keyboard, press the letter next to the correctly spelled word. Scroll the list if necessary.

Other spelling options

The Word Not Found dialog box has several options in addition to Replace Word. Select *Skip Once* to leave the word as it is this one time, *Add to Dictionary* to add the word to the supplemental dictionary, *Edit Word* to edit the word manually (press F7 when done), *Lookup* to look up other words based on your entry, *Ignore Numbers* to skip words that contain numbers, *Select Dictionary* to change to another dictionary. (Medical, legal, foreign language, and other special dictionaries are available from WordPerfect and other sources.)

How much do you want to check?

If you are checking the entire document, the insertion point can be anywhere in the document.

Improving Your Vocabulary

Sometimes the hardest part of writing is selecting just the right word. You may know what you want to say, but you're not sure of the best word. Other times, you find yourself repeating a word frequently in a paragraph and you'd like to find another way to say the same thing without sounding repetitious. These times call for the WordPerfect thesaurus.

To find a synonym:

1. Place the insertion point anywhere in the word you want to replace with a synonym.

2. Select Tools ➤ Writing Tools ➤ Thesaurus to display the Thesaurus dialog box. Several synonyms for the word may be shown in the list boxes.

3. Scroll the list box to highlight the desired word.

4. Select Replace.

Barbara was a serious student.

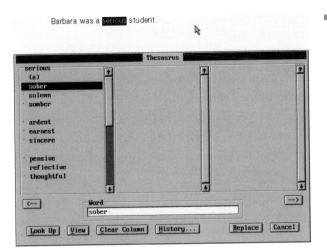

■ *The Thesaurus
dialog box*

 TIP ## More words

Some words in the list box have bullets—large dots—next to them to indicate that the Thesaurus contains additional synonyms for that word.
If none of the words in the list are quite right, you can continue to search for the proper word by highlighting a bulleted word and selecting Lookup.

 TIP ## Word not found

If WordPerfect cannot find a synonym for your word, the message "Word Not Found" will appear. To return to the document, click on OK and select Cancel.

 TIP ## Beware the parts of speech

Depending on the word you are looking up, the thesaurus may list both nouns and verbs, or adjectives. Make sure you replace the word with one of the correct type. Also, select a word that has the same connotation, and avoid using words simply because of their size or novelty. Substituting a simple *I love you, please marry me* with *I philos you, please espouse me* may not make the impression you want.

Improving Your Grammar

WordPerfect's spell checker cannot determine if you used the wrong word when it is correctly spelled. For instance, it won't report that you used *too* instead of *to* or *two*, or used *effect* when you should have used *affect*. Fortunately, WordPerfect includes Grammatik, a powerful program that checks your grammar as well as spelling and punctuation.

To check your grammar:

1. Type or open the document you want checked.

2. Select Tools ➤ Writing Tools ➤ Grammatik.

3. Select Checking ➤ Interactive.

4. Read the description of possible errors and respond using the function keys shown at the bottom of the screen. The figure shows Grammatik checking the preamble of the U.S. Constitution.

5. After the last detected error, select File ➤ Quit to return to WordPerfect.

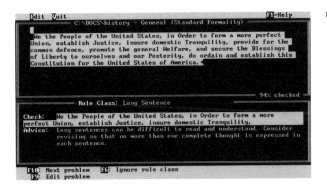

■ *The Grammatik window*

Grammatik commands

The commands displayed at the bottom of the Grammatik window will depend upon the type of error. Press F10 to move onto the next problem, F9 to edit the problem manually (press Esc when done or F9 to recheck the same problem), F7 to add the word to the Grammatik dictionary, F6 to ignore this class of problem, F5 to ignore the phrase, F3 to replace the word or phrase with the suggested replacement and move into the next problem, F2 to replace the word or phrase but stay with the same problem, and Esc to stop the checking process and return to the initial Grammatik menu.

Other Grammatik options

To customize how Grammatik checks for errors, select Preferences from the Grammatik menu. Select Statistics to report on the readability of the document. To review possible mistakes without correcting them, select Checking ➤ Read Only from the initial Grammatik menu.

It's So Easy...

Lesson 17

Using Graphics in Your Documents

As you become familiar with WordPerfect's graphics commands, you'll see that you can create some rather sophisticated documents. Not only can you produce some very dramatic effects, but you can have some fun doing it.

There's really much more to graphics than can be covered in a book of this length, but this lesson will show you the basics you'll need to get started with graphic images in your documents.

Retrieving a Graphic Image

The first step in using a graphic image is to retrieve it into your document. You must know the name of the graphics file, including its file extension, and the drive and directory in which the file is located.

To retrieve a graphic image:

1. Select Graphics ➤ Retrieve Image to display the Retrieve Image File dialog box.

2. Type the name of the image file, then click on OK or press Enter; or select File List, type the path where you store graphics files, then click on OK. Scroll the list, then double-click on the file name you want to retrieve. The image appears in a box on the right of the document, as in the figure.

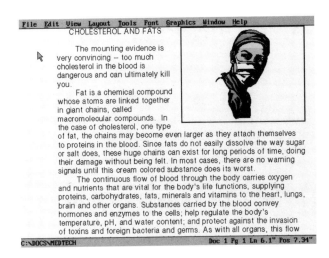

A graphic image
retrieved into document

File not found!

If you see this message, make sure you are typing the correct name
and extension of the file. WordPerfect expects graphics files to be in the
WP60\GRAPHICS directory. If your image is in another directory or
drive, precede the file name with the complete path. If you are retrieving a
WPG file, you do not need to type the extension in the Retrieve Image
File box.

 TIP

Printing graphics

To print graphics, go to the Print dialog box and pull down the Graphics
Quality list under Document Settings. Select High, Medium, or Draft.
High results in the best quality but the slowest printing. Use Draft for
quick draft copies. If you do not have a color printer, screen colors will
print in shades of gray.

Changing the Size and Position of Graphics

You can change the size, shape, and position of a graphics box just as you do for graphic horizontal and vertical lines. With a mouse it's easy.

To change the size and position of graphics:

1. Change to graphics or page view.

2. Click on the graphics box to surround it in a selection box with eight handles.

3. To move the image, point inside the selection box and drag the mouse.

4. To change the size of the box, drag one of the handles.

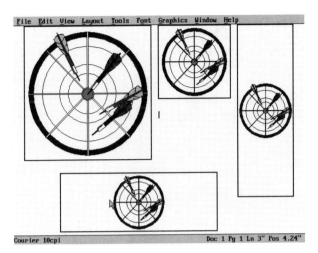

File Edit View Layout Tools Font Graphics Window Help

Courier 10cpi   Doc 1 Pg 1 Ln 3" Pos 4.24"

■ *A graphic in several sizes*

TIP Graphics boxes and images

Think of a graphic as having two separate parts—the image (drawing or picture) itself and the graphics box that surrounds the image. When you change the size of a graphics box, WordPerfect maintains the proper width to height ratio of the image within it, preventing you from distorting the image. If you triple the height of the box without changing the width, for example, the height of the graphic within the box will not change.

TIP To delete a graphics box

Select the graphic, press Del, then select Yes to confirm.

TIP Beyond the screen

You cannot use the mouse to enlarge the graphics box beyond the edge of the screen. To make a larger box, zoom to 50% or 75%, then enlarge the graphic.

Editing a Graphics Box

If you don't care for the plain-vanilla square graphics box, you can customize its appearance. You can change the lines that surround the image, make round rather than square corners, and even have text follow the image's contour.

▪ To edit a graphics box:

1. Double-click on the box, or select the box and select Graphics ➤ Graphics Boxes ➤ Edit to display the Edit Graphics Box dialog box, as shown in the figure.

2. Select options from the Edit Graphics Boxes dialog box.

3. Click on OK.

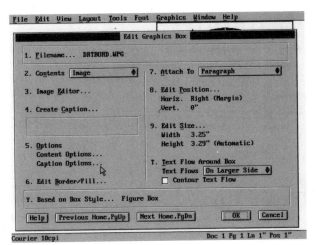

■ *The Edit Graphics Box dialog box*

Read what you need

TIP **Graphics editing options**

Here are some ways to edit your graphic:

— *Following the contour:* Select Contour Text Flow, then OK. The box around the image will disappear and the text will follow the shape of the image.

— *Changing box lines:* Select Edit Border/Fill. A dialog box will appear with options for creating round or square corners, changing line colors, adding a background pattern, changing the box lines, and creating shadow boxes.

— *Flowing text around the box:* By default, text appears on the side of the graphic with the most room between it and the left or right margin. Pull down the Text Flow list to change the position of the text. Options include On Larger Side, Left Side, Right Side, Both Sides, Neither, and Through. Select Through to have text and graphics overlap.

Editing Graphic Images

In addition to editing the graphics box that surrounds the image, you can change the image itself. Experiment with the Image Editor to see how much you can modify a graphic. Editing the graphic changes only how it appears in your document—it does not affect the actual graphics file itself.

To edit the image:

1. Double-click on the graphics box, or select it and select Graphics ➤ Graphic Boxes ➤ Edit.

2. Select Image Editor.

3. Use the menu and button bars on top of the screen and the options on the bottom of the screen to customize the image.

4. Click on Close and on OK to return to the document or click on Cancel to leave the image unchanged.

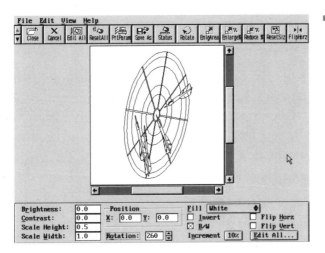

■ *The Image Editor dialog box with a customized graphic*

💡 TIP   Making multiple changes

Each time you make a change to the image, it is redrawn on the screen. To make several changes without having to wait for each redrawing, select Edit All. Make all of the desired changes, then click on OK to redraw the image once.

💡 TIP   Editing images

A thorough discussion of image-editing capabilities requires some knowledge of computer graphics and could fill a book itself. Here are some basics to get you started:

— Press ↑, ↓, ←, and → to move the image within the graphic box.

— Press PgUp and PgDn to scale the image larger and smaller while maintaining the proper height to width ratio.

— Select B/W to convert a color image to black and white.

Rotating Text in Boxes

A graphics text box contains text instead of a graphic image. It is still considered to be a graphics box, because you can change the box size and position using the mouse, which you cannot do to a paragraph in borders (see "Creating Boxed Text" in Lesson 14). But more importantly, you can rotate the text in the box 90, 180, or 270 degrees.

To create a rotated text box:

1. Select Graphics ➤ Graphic Boxes ➤ Create.

2. Select Create Text.

3. Press Alt+F9 to display the Graphics dialog box.

4. Select Rotate Box Contents.

5. Select 0, 90, 180, or 270 degrees and click on OK.

6. Type the text and format it with whatever fonts, sizes, and styles you choose.

7. Press F7.

8. Click on OK.

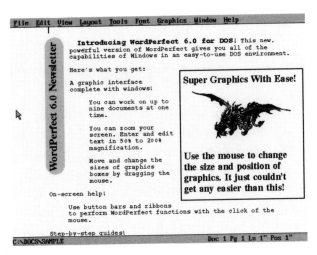

■ *A document showing rotated text in a box with a 20 percent fill, rounded corners, and no border lines and a text box combining text and graphics*

Read what you need

Combining text and graphics

You can combine text and a graphic image in the same box. In the Create Text window, press Alt+F9, select Retrieve Image, then type the path and name of the graphics file.

Reducing box size

The default box size may be much larger than the text within it. Drag the handles to reduce the box size, or use the Edit Graphics Box dialog box—select Edit Sizes, then select Automatic Height and Automatic Width.

Printer compatibility

Some printers may not be able to print rotated graphics in all fonts. Experiment to see what your printer's capabilities are.

Let's Do It!

Even the most powerful features of WordPerfect are easy to use. It just takes a few clicks of the mouse to add lines, borders, and graphics to your document. You can also speed up your work by recording macros that perform functions that you use often. And don't forget to spell check your document and improve it by using the thesaurus and Grammatik.

Once you feel comfortable with these special WordPerfect features, you'll be able to create more varied documents, and you'll work more efficiently and more comfortably.

Adding Lines and Boxes

Graphic lines and borders can add visual interest to your work. In this exercise, we'll get some practice with graphics by creating a letterhead complete with a horizontal line and a shaded page border.

1. Start WordPerfect.

2. Select Font ➤ Font and pull down the Font list.

3. Select a scalable font, such as TrueType, Type 1, or Speedo, if available.

4. Click on OK.

5. Select Font ➤ Size/Position ➤ Very Large.

6. Type your name.

7. Select Font ➤ Size/Position ➤ Normal Size.

8. Press Enter.

9. Select Graphics ➤ Graphics Lines ➤ Create ➤ OK. The default horizontal line appears.

10. Press Enter.

11. Press Alt+F6 for right flush alignment, type your address and telephone number, and press Enter.

Now let's add a custom border around the page.

12. Select Graphics ➤ Borders ➤ Page.

13. Select Fill Style ➤ 20% Shaded Fill ➤ Select.

14. Select Customize ➤ Corners ➤ Round ➤ OK.

15. Click on Close, then click on OK.

16. Select File ➤ Print Preview (or press Shift+F7). Your page should look like Figure 4.1.

17. Select File ➤ Close to return to the document.

18. Select File ➤ Save, type **LHEAD**, and click on OK to save the document.

19. Select File ➤ Print/Fax ➤ Print to print the letterhead.

20. Select File ➤ Close to clear the document from the screen.

21. Select File ➤ Exit WP ➤ Exit if you're not ready to go on.

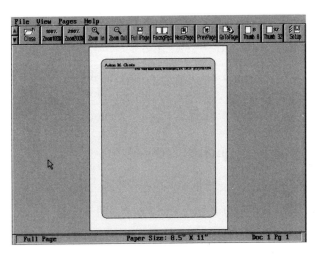

■ FIGURE 4.1:
*The letterhead with a
graphic line and border*

Creating Form Documents

WordPerfect's merge commands make it as easy to mail thousands of letters as it is to create just one. But don't think form letters are useful only for mass mailings. You can use them even if you send just one or two form-type letters per week, such as employment applications or requests for information.

In this exercise we'll create a form letter and envelopes.

Constructing the Data File

The first step is to create a data file containing the variable information you want inserted into the letters. Just follow these steps:

1. Select Tools ➤ Merge ➤ Define ➤ Data [Table].
2. Select Create A Table With Field Names.

Now enter the field names.

3. Type **Name** and press Enter.
4. Type **Address** and press Enter.
5. Type **City** and press Enter.
6. Type **State** and press Enter.
7. Type **Zip** and press Enter.
8. Select OK to display the data table.

Next, enter the information for each copy of the form document.

9. Type **Watson, Inc.** and press Tab.
10. Type **246 Walnut St.** and press Tab.
11. Type **Philadelphia** and press Tab.

12. Type **PA** and press Tab.

13. Type **19101** and press Tab to create a second table row for the next record.

14. Type **Mellow Marshmallow, Inc.** and press Tab.

15. Type **92 Park Ave.** and press Tab.

16. Type **New York** and press Tab.

17. Type **NY** and press Tab.

18. Type **12002**.

19. Select File ➤ Save.

20. Type **MAILLIST** to name the file and click on OK.

21. Select File ➤ Close.

22. Select File ➤ Exit WP ➤ Exit if you're not ready to go on.

Figure 4.2 shows the completed table.

Name	Address	City	State	Zip
Watson, Inc.	246 Walnut St.	Philadelphia	PA	19101
Mellow Marshmallow, Inc.	92 Park Ave.	New York	NY	12002

■ FIGURE 4.2:
The completed data file table

Writing the Form Letter

The second big step is to write the form letter itself, inserting merge codes where you want variable information from the data file to be inserted.

1. Select Tools ➤ Merge ➤ Define ➤ OK ➤ OK.

2. Select Layout ➤ Justification ➤ Center.

3. Type your name and address, then press Enter twice.

4. Select Tools ➤ Date ➤ Code, then press Enter twice.

5. Select Layout ➤ Justification ➤ Left.

Now add the codes to print the address in the merged letters.

6. Press Shift+F9, 1, type **Name**, and click on OK.

7. Press Enter.

8. Press Shift+F9, 1, type **Address**, and click on OK.

9. Press Enter.

10. Press Shift+F9, 1, type **City**, and click on OK.

11. Press , (comma), then press the spacebar.

12. Press Shift+F9, 1, type **State**, and click on OK.

13. Press the spacebar twice.

14. Press Shift+F9, 1, type **Zip**, and click on OK.

15. Press Enter twice.

Finally, complete the letter.

16. Type a short letter:

```
Dear Board of Directors:

        I represent a group of investors in your
company. Please send me a copy of your latest
annual report.

Sincerely,
```

17. Press Enter five times.

18. Type your name. The form letter should now look like Figure 4.3.

19. Select File ➤ Save.

20. Type **REQUEST** to name the file and click on OK.

21. Select File ➤ Close to clear the screen.

22. Select File ➤ Exit ➤ Exit if you're not ready to go on.

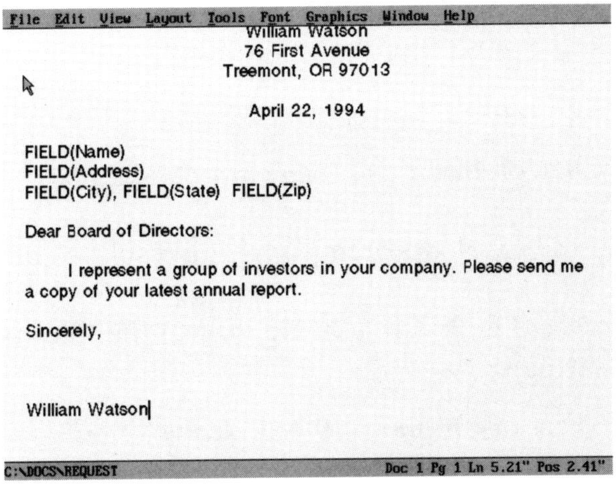

■ FIGURE 4.3:
The completed form letter

Merging Form Letters and Envelopes

To generate the form letters, you just tell WordPerfect the name of the data file and form file. We'll do this in a moment, but first we'll copy the codes that create the address, so you can use the address information in your envelopes and print them along with the letters.

1. Open the Request document.

2. Select the merge codes that represent the address, then select Edit ➤ Copy and Paste (or press Ctrl+Ins).

3. Select File ➤ Close.

4. Select Tools ➤ Merge ➤ Run.

5. Type **REQUEST** in the Form File text box and press Enter.

6. Type **MAILLIST** in the Data File text box and press Enter.

7. Select Data File Options.

8. Select Generate an Envelope for Each Data Record. WordPerfect will display the Envelope dialog box, as in Figure 4.4.

9. Select the Mailing Address box, press Ctrl+V to insert the address codes, and press F7.

10. Select POSTNET Bar Code.

11. Type **Zip**.

12. Click on Insert and then click on Merge.

The letters and envelopes are merged and displayed on the screen.

13. Select File ➤ Close ➤ No to clear the screen without saving.

14. Select File ➤ Exit WP ➤ Exit.

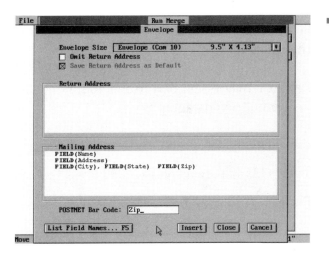

Macros

If you do much typing, you'll find yourself repeating the same series of keystrokes time and again—typing your letterhead, applying a certain format, adding page numbers or graphic elements. You can save time by creating macros to automate these chores.

Let's create and use two macros, starting with a macro that inserts your letterhead and date.

1. Select Tools ➤ Macro ➤ Record (or press Ctrl+F10).

2. Press Alt+L to assign a shortcut key combination to the macro, and click on OK. Now you're ready to record the actual keystrokes of the macro.

3. Select Layout ➤ Justification ➤ Center.

4. Type your name and address and press Enter.

5. Select Tools ➤ Date ➤ Code and press Enter.

6. Select Layout ➤ Justification ➤ Left.

7. Press Enter twice.

8. Select Tools ➤ Macro ➤ Stop (or press Ctrl+F10) to save the macro.

Next we'll create a macro that performs a common editing task—swapping the position of two paragraphs.

9. Type **This is paragraph one** and press Enter.

10. Type **This is paragraph two** and press Enter.

11. Place the insertion point anywhere in the second paragraph.

12. Select Tools ➤ Macro ➤ Record, press Alt+S to assign a shortcut key combination, and click on OK. The following keystrokes will be included in the macro.

13. Select Edit ➤ Select ➤ Paragraph.

14. Select Edit ➤ Cut and Paste (or press Ctrl+Del) to delete the paragraph and place it into the Clipboard.

15. Press Ctrl+↑ and press Home to move the insertion point to the beginning of the first paragraph. (Pressing Home insures that this macro will work with an indented paragraph.)

16. Select Edit ➤ Paste (or press Ctrl+V) to insert the deleted paragraph.

17. Select Tools ➤ Macro ➤ Stop (or press Ctrl+F10) to save the macro.

18. Select File ➤ Close ➤ No.

Using Macros

By linking a macro with an Alt-key combination, you can play it instantly—you don't have to pull down a menu or use a dialog box. Let's try this using the Alt+L and Alt+S macros you just created.

1. Press Alt+L.

Your address appears on the screen just as you typed it. You could also have run the macro by selecting ALTL in the Macro Play dialog box. Now we'll try using the Swap macro.

2. Type **I want this to be the second paragraph**, and press Enter.

3. Type **I want this to be the first paragraph**, and press Enter.

4. Place the insertion point in the second paragraph.

5. Press Alt+S.

The Swap macro is recalled from the disk and run, switching the two paragraphs.

6. Select File ➤ Close ➤ No to clear the document window.

Writing Tools

Even if you rarely use most features of WordPerfect, you'll find the speller and thesaurus to be invaluable. In fact, many writers believe these to be the most useful tools that WordPerfect provides.

Speller

It's a good idea to get into the habit of spell checking every document before you print it. It doesn't take very long and it can save you quite a few headaches.

Let's practice using the speller. We'll type a short document—riddled with errors—and let WordPerfect help correct it.

1. Type the following paragraphs exactly as they appear. Be sure to type in any spelling and typographical errors.

```
    Nellie Watson, former burlesq leading lady
and wife of show operator and star Sliding Billy
WAtson, was shot and killed at at the Three
Hundred Club on April 7, 1926.
    Mrs. Watson, who retirred from burlesque in
1918, appeared with her husband in Girls from
Happyland between 1910 and 1911.
```

2. Select Tools ➤ Writing Tools ➤ Speller.

3. Select Document.

WordPerfect finds the first possible error and displays the dialog box shown in Figure 4.5. In this case, the name *Nellie* is not in WordPerfect's dictionary. The word will become highlighted in the text and suggested spellings will appear in the Suggestions list box.

4. Since the word is spelled correctly, select Skip in this Document.

5. WordPerfect continues checking the document until it finds the next unknown word, *burlesq.* The correct spelling of the word is shown highlighted in the list box. Double-click on the word *burlesque* in the list box, or select Replace Word.

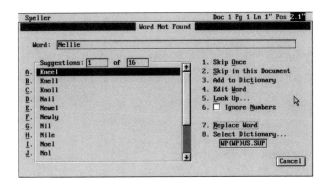

■ FIGURE 4.5:
The Spelling dialog box

6. The next error located is the capitalization in *WAtson*. Select Replace Word to correctly lowercase the second letter in the word.

WordPerfect now detects the repetition of the word *at*. A dialog box appears with options to continue and accept both words or to delete the second occurrence.

7. Select Delete Duplicate Word. The next word found is *retirred*.

8. Double-click on the word retired in the list box or select Replace Word.

Finally, WordPerfect stops at the word *Happyland*. WordPerfect cannot find any alternative spellings for this word, so it displays the message "Word Not Found" in the status bar. Let's add the word to the dictionary so it will no longer be reported as a possible error.

9. Select Add. The word will be inserted in the file WP{WP}US.SUP. This is a supplemental dictionary file where you can store words that you want WordPerfect to accept as correct.

10. A box appears with the message "Spell Check Completed" indicating that the entire document has been checked. Click on OK.

Thesaurus

Use the thesaurus when you can't think of an appropriate word or when you find yourself using the same word over and over again. But make your selections wisely—don't choose words just because they're long or unusual.

Let's look for a synonym for the word *former* in the document you used for the spelling check.

1. Place the insertion point anywhere in the word *former*. If you do not still have the document on the screen, just type the word **former**.

2. Select Tools ➤ Writing Tools ➤ Thesaurus to display the Thesaurus dialog box.

Several synonyms for the word *former* are shown in the list box on the left. WordPerfect will use the other, now empty, list boxes when necessary.

3. Scroll down the list box. At the bottom, you'll see two antonyms for *former*—*future* and *modern*.

4. Scroll back up to highlight the word *past*, then select Replace. The word *past* replaces *former* in the document.

5. Select File ➤ Close ➤ No to clear the screen without saving.

6. Select File ➤ Exit WP ➤ Exit if you're not ready to go on.

Working with Graphics

A well-chosen graphic image can transform the look of your document. But as with lines and borders, don't overdo it with graphics. Avoid graphics that have no relation to the text or that will distract from your words rather than support them.

For practice, let's add a graphic image to a document. We'll use GLOBE.WPG, a graphic file supplied with WordPerfect in the WP60\GRAPHICS directory.

1. Type the following:

   > The city of Berlin evokes visions of conquering armies, intrigue, and the changing political tide that swept through Europe. It is unfortunate that these impressions mask the true nature of the city. Berlin is a city of diversity, culture, and science.
   >
   > Berlin dates to the 13th century when it was a busy reloading point along the Elbe-Havel-Spree waterway. Over the years, the city gained prominence through an association with the Hanseatic League. In 1443, Frederick II built a palace on an island in the Spree, marking the start of Berlin's reign as capital.

2. Select File ➤ Save, type **BERLIN**, and click on OK.

3. Press Home, Home, ↑ to move the insertion point to the start of the document.

4. If you are not in graphics view, change to it now.

5. Select Graphics ➤ Retrieve Image.

6. Type **GLOBE** and click on OK. The graphic appears in a box on the right of the screen.

Now let's see how the graphic appears with text following its contour.

7. Click in the graphics box to select it.

8. Drag the box down, so it is below the level of the second line in the paragraph.

9. Double-click on the graphics box to display the Edit Graphics Boxes dialog box.

10. Select Contour Text Flow.

11. Click on OK.

The lines around the box disappear and WordPerfect adjusts the text to follow the shape of the graphic. Your document should look like Figure 4.6.

Now, let's reinstate the box lines, create a shadow box and rotate the globe 45 degrees.

12. Double-click on the graphic image.

13. Select Contour Text Flow to turn off this feature.

14. Select Edit Border/Fill.

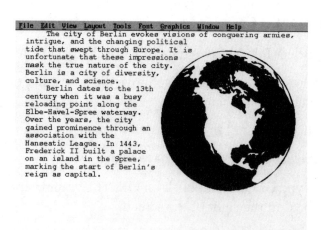

■ FIGURE 4.6:
Text following the contour of GLOBE.WPG

15. Select Shadow ➤ Lower Right ➤ OK ➤ Close.

16. Select Image Editor.

17. Select Rotation, type **45**, press Enter, and select Close.

18. Click on OK to return to the document. It should now look like Figure 4.7.

19. Select File ➤ Save.

20. Select File ➤ Print/Fax ➤ Print.

21. Select File ➤ Close.

22. Select File ➤ Exit WP ➤ Exit.

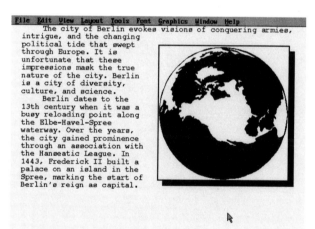

■ FIGURE 4.7:
The edited graphics box and image

INDEX

Boldface page numbers indicate primary references and explanations

Italic page numbers refer to figures

C

Boldface page numbers indicate primary references and explanations

Italic page numbers refer to figures

for parallel columns, 220–221
for size of table columns, 212
cursor, 5. *See also* insertion point
cursor-movement keys, 49
cursor position in status bar, 4
Custom Widths parallel columns
    option, 220
customizing
    borders, 230, 232
    button bars, **248–249**
    date formats, **90–91**
    page numbers, **188–189**
Cut option, 57, 75
Cut and Paste option, 74, 116–117
Cyrillic character set, 140

D

dashes (-)
    in formulas, 168, 215
    for hyphens, 168
    printing lines of, 93
data files
    for envelopes, 242
    for form letters, **236–237**, *237*, 241
    practice with, 270–272, *271*
data in tables, entering, **208–209**, *209*
Data [Table] option, 236
Data [Text] option, 237
Date Code button, 87
Date dialog box, 86, *87*
Date Format button, 89
Date Format dialog box, 91
Date Formats dialog box, 88, *89*
Date options, 86, 88, 90
Date Text button, 87
dates

formats for, **88–91**
    inserting, **86–87**, *87*, 123–124
decimal tabs, 156, **158–159**, *159*
defaults
    for button bars, 24–25
    for date format, 88
    for envelopes, 179
    for lines, 224
    for magnification, 98
    for margins, 171
    for page size, 177
    for paragraph format, 161
    for printing, 32
    for repeating keystrokes, 93
    for tabs, 156
Define option
    for data files, 236–237
    for form letters, 238
definitions in Help system, 21
Del key
    for deleting text, 56–57
    for freehand lines, 229
Delete option, 57
Delete and Append option, 81
Delete Duplicate Word option, 279
Delete Row: option, 210
deleting
    dates, 87
    format codes, 136
    freehand lines, 229
    graphics boxes, 261
    graphics lines, 227
    hard page breaks, 95
    headers and footers, 182
    hyphens, 167
    list boxes, 8

Boldface page numbers indicate primary references and explanations

Italic page numbers refer to figures

Boldface page numbers indicate primary references and explanations

Italic page numbers refer to figures

Boldface page numbers indicate primary references and explanations

Boldface page numbers indicate primary references and explanations

Italic page numbers refer to figures

Boldface page numbers indicate primary references and explanations

Italic page numbers refer to figures

Boldface page numbers indicate primary references and explanations

Boldface page numbers indicate primary references and explanations

Italic page numbers refer to figures

Italic page numbers refer to figures

Italic page numbers refer to figures

SYBEX

FREE BROCHURE!

Complete this form today, and we'll send you a full-color brochure of Sybex bestsellers.

Please supply the name of the Sybex book purchased.

_____

How would you rate it?

_____ Excellent   _____ Very Good   _____ Average   _____ Poor

Why did you select this particular book?

_____ Recommended to me by a friend
_____ Recommended to me by store personnel
_____ Saw an advertisement in _____
_____ Author's reputation
_____ Saw in Sybex catalog
_____ Required textbook
_____ Sybex reputation
_____ Read book review in _____
_____ In-store display
_____ Other _____

Where did you buy it?

_____ Bookstore
_____ Computer Store or Software Store
_____ Catalog (name: _____)
_____ Direct from Sybex
_____ Other: _____

Did you buy this book with your personal funds?

_____ Yes   _____ No

About how many computer books do you buy each year?

_____ 1-3   _____ 3-5   _____ 5-7   _____ 7-9   _____ 10+

About how many Sybex books do you own?

_____ 1-3   _____ 3-5   _____ 5-7   _____ 7-9   _____ 10+

Please indicate your level of experience with the software covered in this book:

_____ Beginner   _____ Intermediate   _____ Advanced

Which types of software packages do you use regularly?

_____ Accounting	_____ Databases	_____ Networks
_____ Amiga	_____ Desktop Publishing	_____ Operating Systems
_____ Apple/Mac	_____ File Utilities	_____ Spreadsheets
_____ CAD	_____ Money Management	_____ Word Processing
_____ Communications	_____ Languages	_____ Other _____
		(please specify)

Which of the following best describes your job title?

_____ Administrative/Secretarial   _____ President/CEO

_____ Director   _____ Manager/Supervisor

_____ Engineer/Technician   _____ Other _____
(please specify)

Comments on the weaknesses/strengths of this book: _____

_____

_____

_____

_____

Name _____

Street _____

City/State/Zip _____

Phone _____

PLEASE FOLD, SEAL, AND MAIL TO SYBEX

SYBEX, INC.
Department M
2021 CHALLENGER DR.
ALAMEDA, CALIFORNIA USA
94501

SYBEX

Function-Key Shortcuts

KEYSTROKE(S)	EFFECT
F1	Displays context-sensitive help
Ctrl+F1	Shells temporarily to DOS
Alt+F1	Displays menus of writing tools
Shift+F1	Sets up WordPerfect default settings
F2	Searches forward through a document
Ctrl+F2	Begins the spell check process
Alt+F2	Replaces text
Shift+F2	Searches backward through a document
F3	Switches to other document windows
Ctrl+F3	Displays screen and display options
Alt+F3	Reveals codes
Shift+F3	Switches to the previous document
F4	Indents the paragraph on the left
Ctrl+F4	Displays the Move dialog box
Alt+F4	Turns on the block functions for selecting text
Shift+F4	Indents paragraphs on the left and right
F5	Displays the File Manager
Ctrl+F5	Turns on automatic outline features
Alt+F5	Marks text for an index, table of contents and table of authorities
Shift+F5	Inserts date and changes date formats
F6	Formats text in boldface
Ctrl+F6	Creates a decimal-aligned tab stop
Alt+F6	Justifies text on the right
Shift+F6	Centers text between the left and right margins
F7	Exits the current document window
Ctrl+F7	Inserts footnotes and endnotes
Alt+F7	Creates tables and columns
Shift+F7	Prints and faxes documents
F8	Underlines text
Ctrl+F8	Displays the Font dialog box
Alt+F8	Creates and selects styles for formatting
Shift+F8	Displays format and layout options